ROYAL COUR

The Royal Court Theatre presents

THE VILLAGE BIKE

by Penelope Skinner

THE VILLAGE BIKE was first performed at the Royal Court Jerwood Theatre Upstairs, Sloane Square, London on Friday 24th June 2011.

Jerwood New Playwrights is supported by:

JERWOOD CHARITABLE FOUNDATION

Principal Sponsor

Coutts

THE VILLAGE BIKE

by Penelope Skinner

in order of appearance
Becky **Romola Garai**
John **Nicholas Burns**
Jenny **Alexandra Gilbreath**
Mike **Phil Cornwell**
Oliver **Dominic Rowan**
Alice **Sasha Waddell**

Director **Joe Hill-Gibbins**
Designer **Helen Goddard**
Lighting Designer **James Farncombe**
Sound Designer **David McSeveney**
Casting Director **Amy Ball**
Assistant Director **Rachel Bagshaw**
Production Manager **Tariq Rifaat**
Stage Managers **Julia Slienger, Alison Rich**
Costume Supervisor **Iona Kenrick**
Stage Management Work Placement **Charlotte Bayford**
Set built by **Footprint Scenery Ltd**

The Royal Court and Stage Management wish to thank to following for their help with this production: Ben Delfont, Bishop's Move, Britania Movers, Donmar Warehouse, Harmony, Marks & Spencers, Nivea, Peter Jones, Russell Hobbs, Tesco.

THE COMPANY

PENELOPE SKINNER (Writer)

FOR THE ROYAL COURT: The Literary Ball (International Rough Cut).

OTHER PLAYS INCLUDE: Greenland (co-writer, National); Eigengrau (Bush); Fucked (Old Red Lion/Assembly Rooms Edinburgh).

AWARDS INCLUDE: 2011 George Devine Award for Most Promising Playwright.

Penelope Skinner was a member of the Royal Court Young Writers Programme.

RACHEL BAGSHAW (Assistant Director)

AS ASSISTANT DIRECTOR THEATRE INCLUDES: The Glass Menagerie (Young Vic); Small Craft Warnings (RADA); Flower Girls (Graeae/New Wolsey Theatre, Ipswich); There Came a Gypsy Riding (Almeida); Eighty Days Around the World (Lawrence Batley Theatre).

AS DIRECTOR THEATRE INCLUDES: Remember How to Fly (Young Vic); The Rhinestone Rollers, Just Me, Bell (Graeae); Not Not Not Not Not Enough Oxygen (Cockpit Theatre); All Shook Up (Pyramid Theatre Company); Splendour (Cockpit Theatre); bash (Mountview Academy).

Rachel is Resident Assistant Director (ACE) at the Young Vic.

NICHOLAS BURNS (John)

THEATRE INCLUDES: Ghost Stories (Lyric Hammersmith/West End); Fat Pig (West End); Much Ado About Nothing (Sheffield Crucible); Arcadia (Bristol Old Vic/Birmingham Rep); Two Gentleman of Verona, A Midsummer Night's Dream (Regent's Park); The Madness of George Dubya (Teatro Teknis/Pleasance/Arts Theatre); The Taming of the Shrew (Nottingham Playhouse).

TELEVISION INCLUDES: Psychoville, The Sinking of the Laconia, Misfits, Mister Eleven, Monday Monday, No Heroics, Other People, Never Better, The IT Crowd, Roman's Empire, Miss Marple, Benidorm, London, Fear of Fanny, Modern Men, Nighty Night, Man Stroke Woman, The Mighty Boosh, Nathan Barley, Swiss Tony, A Touch of Frost, Absolute Power, Manchild, Cambridge Spies, Eastenders, The House That Jack Built, The Bill, Surrealissimo, Swivel on the Tip.

PHIL CORNWELL (Mike)

THEATRE INCLUDES: Birthday Party, Look Back in Anger (ESTA); I Could Never Be Your Woman (Could Never Ltd); Journey's End (Background); Outbreak of God in Area 9 (Young Vic); Small Expectations (QEH); Wasp 05 (Jelly Roll Prods.); A View from the Bridge (Bankside).

TELEVISION INCLUDES: Skins, Game Over, Harry and Paul, The Legend of Dick and Dom, Missing, Omid 'B', Hotel Trubble, Dani's House, Doctor Who, Headcases, Harry and Paul, MI High, Phoo Action, The Shadow in the North, Dead Ringers, The Comic Strop Series, Dunkirk, I'm Alan Partridge, The Bill, Holby City, Murder in Mind, Clocking Off, Happiness, World of Pub, Stella Street, Fun at the Funeral Party, Sunburn, Gormenghast, Only Fools and Horses, Trial and Retribution, Big Train.

FILM INCLUDES: Cockneys Versus Zombies, Made in Dagenham, Lady Godiva: Back in the Saddle, I Could Never Be Your Woman, Scoop, Colour Me Kubrick, Chromophobia, Churchill: The Hollywood Years, Large, Blood, Out of Depth, Stella Street: The Movie.

RADIO INCLUDES: Polly Oaks, The Cornwall Estate, 28 Acts in 28 Minutes, And This is Them, Blue Jam, Cinema Scrapbook, First Impressions, Front Row, King of The Road, Lenin of The Rovers, Loose Ends, Mango, Night Cap, Overtime, Remember Live Aid, Spoilsports, The Comedy Controller, The Day the Music Died, The Pits, Watch With Monkey, Weekending.

JAMES FARNCOMBE (Lighting Designer)

FOR THE ROYAL COURT: Wanderlust, Blest be the Tie, What's in the Cat.

OTHER THEATRE INCLUDES: Men Should Weep (National); The Glass Menagerie (Young Vic); The Overcoat (Gecko/Lyric Hammersmith); Juliet and Her Romeo, Swallows and Amazons, Far Away (Bristol Old Vic); Kommilitonen (Royal Academy of Music/Julliard School, New York); The Whiskey Taster, Like a Fishbone (Bush); Dancing at Lughnasa, Little Shop of Horrors (Birmingham Rep); A Day in the Death of Joe Egg, Breaking the Silence (Nottingham Playhouse); Ghost Stories (Liverpool Playhouse/Lyric Hammersmith/West End/Toronto); Private Fears in Public Places (Northampton Theatre Royal); The Great Game (Tricycle Theatre/US tour); The Winter's Tale (Schtanhaus/Headlong); Twisted Tales (Lyric Theatre, Hammersmith); Oleanna (Nottingham Lakeside); Plenty (Sheffield Crucible Studio).

AWARDS INCLUDE: Whitelight Best Lighting Design, Whatsonstage Awards 2011.

James is a design associate at the Bush Theatre, London.

ROMOLA GARAI (Becky)

THEATRE INCLUDES: Three Sisters (Filter/Lyric Hammersmith); King Lear/The Seagull (RSC); Calico (West End).

TELEVISION INCLUDES: The Hour, Crimson Petal and the White, Mary Bryant, Daniel Deronda, Perfect, Attachments, The Blonde Bombshells.

FILM INCLUDES: One Day, 1939, The Other Man, Atonement, Angel, Amazing Grace, Scoop, As You Like It, Inside I'm Dancing, Vanity Fair, Havana Nights, Nicholas Nickleby, I Capture the Castle.

ALEXANDRA GILBREATH (Jenny)

FOR THE ROYAL COURT: Disappeared.

OTHER THEATRE INCLUDES: Hay Fever (Rose); Twelfth Night, As You Like It, The Merry Wives of Windsor, The Tamer Tamed, The Taming of the Shrew, Romeo and Juliet, The Winter's Tale, Cyrano de Bergerac, Ghosts (RSC); The House of Bernarda Alba (Gate); Hedda Gabler (ETC).

TELEVISION & FILM INCLUDES: Dead Babies, Inspector George Gently, Casualty, Trial and Retribution, Life Begins, Absolute Power, The Commander, The Waltz King, Happiness, Midsomer Murders, The Bill, The Project, Monarch of the Glen, Out of Hours, A Wing and a Prayer.

AWARDS: Ian Charleson Award.

HELEN GODDARD (Designer)

THEATRE INCLUDES: The Years Between (Northampton Theatre Royal); Lakeboat, Prairie du Chien (Arcola); Lulu, Dream Story (Gate); Comedians, Looking for Buddy (Octagon Bolton); And a Nightingale Sang (New Vic Theatre/Scarborough/Oldham Coliseum); James and the Giant Peach, Mickey Salberg's Crystal Ballroom Dance Band, Mira Mira, The Siren's Call, (Watermill Theatre); Public Property, Lovely and Misfit - Tennessee William short plays, Well (Trafalgar Studios); Knives in Hens (Bath Theatre Royal); Let There Be Love (Tricycle); GBS, The Lifesavers, The Ones That Flutter (Theatre 503); The Roaring Girl (Bristol Old Vic).

AWARDS: Linbury Prize for Stage Design 2007 for Let There Be Love.

JOE HILL-GIBBINS (Director)

FOR THE ROYAL COURT: The Girlfriend Experience (Young Vic and Royal Court/Drum Theatre Plymouth), Bliss, Family Plays, A Girl in a Car with a Man.

OTHER THEATRE INCLUDES: The Glass Menagerie, The Beauty Queen of Leenane, A Respectable Wedding (Young Vic); The Fever (Theatre503 in association with the Young Vic); A Thought in Three Parts (BAC).

AWARDS INCLUDE: James Menzies-Kitchin Trust Young Director's Award-winner for A Thought in Three Parts.

Joe is Deputy Artistic Director of the Young Vic.

DAVID McSEVENEY (Sound Designer)

David trained at the Central School of Speech and Drama completing a BA Hons. in Theatre Practice (Sound Design).

FOR THE ROYAL COURT: Clybourne Park (& West End), Ingredient X, Posh, Disconnect, Cock, A Miracle, The Stone, Shades, 7 Jewish Children, The Girlfriend Experience (& Theatre Royal Plymouth & Young Vic), Contractions, Fear & Misery/War & Peace.

OTHER THEATRE INCLUDES: The Tin Horizon (Theatre 503); Gaslight (Old Vic); Charley's Aunt, An Hour and a Half Late (Theatre Royal Bath); A Passage to India, After Mrs Rochester, Madame Bovary (Shared Experience); Men Should Weep, Rookery Nook (Oxford Stage Company); Othello (Southwark Playhouse).

AS ASSISTANT DESIGNER: The Permanent Way (Out of Joint); My Brilliant Divorce, Auntie and Me (West End); Accidental Death of an Anarchist (Donmar).

David is Head of Sound at the Royal Court.

DOMINIC ROWAN (Oliver)

FOR THE ROYAL COURT: Way to Heaven, Forty Winks.

THEATRE INCLUDES: Henry VIII, A New World, As You Like It (Shakespeare's Globe); The Misanthrope, Under the Blue Sky (West End); The Spanish Tragedy (Arcola); After Dido (ENO/Young Vic); Happy Now?, Dream Play, Iphegina at Aulis, Mourning Becomes Electra, Three Sisters, The Talking Cure, Private Lives (National); A Voyage Round My Father, Lobby Hero (Donmar); The Importance of Being Earnest (Oxford Playhouse); Sexual Perversity in Chicago (Sheffield Crucible); Merchant of Venice, Two Gentlemen of Verona, Talk of the City (RSC).

TELEVISION INCLUDES: Law and Order, Catwalk Dogs, Baby Boom, Trial and Retribution, The Lavender List, The Family Man, Rescue Me, Lost World, Swallow, North Square, Hearts and Bones, A Rather English Marriage, Between the Lines, Alan Dosser, Devil's Advocate, No Bananas, Emma, The Tennant of Wildfell Hall.

FILM: The Tulse Luper Suitcases.

SASHA WADDELL (Alice)

THEATRE INCLUDES: Eight Women (Southwark Playhouse); Duet for One, Donkeys Years, Fallen Angels, Out of Order (Vienna's English Theatre); Lady Windermere's Fan (Chichester Festival Theatre); Twelfth Night (RSC); The Mousetrap (St. Martin's Theatre); The Young Idea (Chester Gateway); Dear Brutus (King's Head); Candida (UK tour); The Winter's Tale, Twelfth Night (Creation Theatre); Private Lives (Margate Theatre Royal); Scenes from a Marriage, The Learned Ladies (Tristan Bates Theatre); Equiano (Oval House/UK tour).

TELEVISION INCLUDES: Holby City, Julian Fellowes Investigates: The Case of the Earl of Erroll, Krakatoa, A Lump in my Throat, The People's Princess, Gobble.

FILM INCLUDES: Ealing Comedy.

THE ENGLISH STAGE COMPANY AT THE ROYAL COURT THEATRE

'For me the theatre is really a religion or way of life. You must decide what you feel the world is about and what you want to say about it, so that everything in the theatre you work in is saying the same thing ... A theatre must have a recognisable attitude. It will have one, whether you like it or not.'

George Devine, first artistic director of the English Stage Company: notes for an unwritten book.

photo: Stephen Cummiskey

As Britain's leading national company dedicated to new work, the Royal Court Theatre produces new plays of the highest quality, working with writers from all backgrounds, and asking questions about who we are and the world in which we live.

"The Royal Court has been at the centre of British cultural life for the past 50 years, an engine room for new writing and constantly transforming the theatrical culture." Stephen Daldry

Since its foundation in 1956, the Royal Court has presented premieres by almost every leading contemporary British playwright, from John Osborne's Look Back in Anger to Caryl Churchill's A Number and Tom Stoppard's Rock 'n' Roll. Just some of the other writers to have chosen the Royal Court to premiere their work include Edward Albee, John Arden, Richard Bean, Samuel Beckett, Edward Bond, Leo Butler, Jez Butterworth, Martin Crimp, Ariel Dorfman, Stella Feehily, Christopher Hampton, David Hare, Eugène Ionesco, Ann Jellicoe, Terry Johnson, Sarah Kane, David Mamet, Martin McDonagh, Conor McPherson, Joe Penhall, Lucy Prebble, Mark Ravenhill, Simon Stephens, Wole Soyinka, Polly Stenham, David Storey, Debbie Tucker Green, Arnold Wesker and Roy Williams.

"It is risky to miss a production there." Financial Times

In addition to its full-scale productions, the Royal Court also facilitates international work at a grass roots level, developing exchanges which bring young writers to Britain and sending British writers, actors and directors to work with artists around the world. The research and play development arm of the Royal Court Theatre, The Studio, finds the most exciting and diverse range of new voices in the UK. The Studio runs play-writing groups including the Young Writers Programme, Critical Mass for black, Asian and minority ethnic writers and the biennial Young Writers Festival. For further information, go to http://www.royalcourttheatre.com/playwriting.

"Yes, the Royal Court is on a roll. Yes, Dominic Cooke has just the genius and kick that this venue needs... It's fist-bitingly exciting." Independent

JERWOOD CHARITABLE FOUNDATION

Since 1994 Jerwood New Playwrights has contributed to 69 new plays at the Royal Court including Joe Penhall's SOME VOICES, Mark Ravenhill's SHOPPING AND FUCKING (co-production with Out of Joint), Ayub Khan Din's EAST IS EAST (co-production with Tamasha), Martin McDonagh's THE BEAUTY QUEEN OF LEENANE (co-production with Druid Theatre Company), Conor McPherson's THE WEIR, Nick Grosso's REAL CLASSY AFFAIR, Sarah Kane's 4.48 PSYCHOSIS, Gary Mitchell's THE FORCE OF CHANGE, David Eldridge's UNDER THE BLUE SKY, David Harrower's PRESENCE, Simon Stephens' HERONS, Roy Williams' CLUBLAND, Leo Butler's REDUNDANT, Michael Wynne's THE PEOPLE ARE FRIENDLY, David Greig's OUTLYING ISLANDS, Zinnie Harris' NIGHTINGALE AND CHASE, Grae Cleugh's FUCKING GAMES, Rona Munro's IRON, Richard Bean's UNDER THE WHALEBACK, Ché Walker's FLESH WOUND, Roy Williams' FALLOUT, Mick Mahoney's FOOD CHAIN, Ayub Khan Din's NOTES ON FALLING LEAVES, Leo Butler's LUCKY DOG, Simon Stephens' COUNTRY MUSIC, Laura Wade's BREATHING CORPSES, Debbie Tucker Green's STONING MARY, David Eldridge's INCOMPLETE AND RANDOM ACTS OF KINDNESS, Gregory Burke's ON TOUR, Stella Feehily's O GO MY MAN, Simon Stephens' MOTORTOWN, Simon Farquhar's RAINBOW KISS, April de Angelis, Stella Feehily, Tanika Gupta, Chloe Moss and Laura Wade's CATCH, Mike Bartlett's MY CHILD, Polly Stenham's THAT FACE, Alexi Kaye Campbell's THE PRIDE, Fiona Evans' SCARBOROUGH, Levi David Addai's OXFORD STREET, Bola Agbaje's GONE TOO FAR!, Alia Bano's SHADES, Polly Stenham's TUSK TUSK and Tim Crouch's THE AUTHOR.

In 2010, Jerwood New Playwrights supported Bola Agbaje's OFF THE ENDZ, DC Moore's THE EMPIRE and Anya Reiss' SPUR OF THE MOMENT. So far in 2011 Jerwood New Playwrights has supported Anya Reiss' THE ACID TEST. Jerwood New Playwrights is supported by the Jerwood Charitable Foundation.

The Jerwood Charitable Foundation is dedicated to imaginative and responsible revenue funding of the arts, supporting artists to develop and grow at important stages in their careers. They work with artists across art forms, from dance and theatre to literature, music and the visual arts. www.jerwoodcharitablefoundation.org.

Anya Reiss' THE ACID TEST
(photo: Manuel Harlan)

Bola Agbaje's OFF THE ENDZ
(photo: Johan Persson)

MAKING IT HAPPEN

The Royal Court develops and produces more new plays than any other national theatre in the UK. To produce such a broad and eclectic programme and all of our play development activities costs over £5 million every year. Just under half of this is met by principal funding from Arts Council England. The rest must be found from box office income, trading and financial support from private individuals, companies and charitable foundations. The Royal Court is a registered charity (231242) and grateful for every donation it receives towards its work.

You can support the theatre by joining one of its membership schemes or by making a donation towards the Writers Development Fund. The Fund underpins all of the work that the Royal Court undertakes with new and emerging playwrights across the globe, giving them the tools and opportunities to flourish.

MAJOR PARTNERSHIPS

The Royal Court is able to offer its unique playwriting and audience development programmes because of significant and longstanding partnerships with the organisations that support it.

Coutts & Co is the Principal Sponsor of the Royal Court. The Genesis Foundation supports the Royal Court's work with International Playwrights. Theatre Local is sponsored by Bloomberg. The Jerwood Charitable Foundation supports new plays by playwrights through the Jerwood New Playwrights series. The Artistic Director's Chair is supported by a lead grant from The Peter Jay Sharp Foundation, contributing to the activities of the Artistic Director's office. Over the past ten years the BBC has supported the Gerald Chapman Fund for directors.

The Harold Pinter Playwright's Award is given annually by his widow, Lady Antonia Fraser, to support a new commission at the Royal Court.

DEVELOPMENT ADVOCATES

Supported by
**ARTS COUNCIL
ENGLAND**

PROGRAMME SUPPORTERS

We've always been happy to be less famous than our clients

Throughout our long history, Coutts has always been happy to be less famous than our clients. Clients such as Sir Henry Irving, Phineas Barnum, Bram Stoker, Charles Dickens and Frederic Chopin to name but a few.

Coutts has a long and rich association with the performing arts, and we are still privileged to have many individuals from this arena amongst our clients. As a leading sponsor of the performing arts, Coutts is pleased and proud to support the Royal Court.

For more information about Coutts, please call us on 020 7753 1365 or visit our website www.coutts.com

Sir Henry Irving was considered to be one of the greatest actors of his day. He played a wide range of Shakespearean roles and was a good friend of Thomas Coutts' granddaughter.

Principal Sponsor

Penelope Skinner

The Village Bike

faber and faber

First published in 2011
by Faber and Faber Limited
74–77 Great Russell Street, London WC1B 3DA

Typeset by Country Setting, Kingsdown, Kent CT14 8ES
Printed and bound by CPI Group (UK) Ltd, Croydon, CR0 4YY

A CIP record for this book
is available from the British Library

ISBN 978-0-571-27948-7

6 8 10 9 7

For Claire C

Acknowledgements

Leo Butler and the Royal Court Young Writers
Super Group 2009. Dominic Cooke and everyone at the
Royal Court, especially Jeremy Herrin, Clare McQuillan,
Marcello dos Santos and Nic Wass. The actors who took
part in the read-through in December 2009. The cast and
crew: Joe Hill-Gibbins, Helen Goddard, Rachel Bagshaw,
Romola Garai, Nicholas Burns, Dominic Rowan,
Alex Gilbreath, Phil Cornwell and Sasha Waddell.
Giles Smart and Andy Gout at United. Dinah Wood
and Steve King at Faber. Ruth Little, Aaron Paterson,
Natalie Donbavand, Ben James, Alison O'Donnell,
Janfarie Skinner, Andrew Skinner, Andy Skinner,
Ginny Vollenweider, Victoria Ward, Tim Hoare,
Polly Findlay, Faith Miles, Janet and Christopher
Ridsdill-Smith and Jamie Mattless.

Special thanks to Emma Crowe, for telling me
what the play was really about and how to fix it.
And for cycling eighteen miles.

Characters

Becky
early thirties

John
early thirties

Jenny
early forties

Oliver
mid-forties

Alice
early forties

Mike
early fifties

Setting

The play takes places in three cottages
in a village somewhere in middle England,
at the height of summer.

Becky and John's cottage is old, but
halfway through being renovated and modernised.
It is on two levels. On the top level, the bedroom,
with a door into the bathroom. Downstairs,
the kitchen. In the kitchen, a stereo. There is
a door leading to the back garden.

Around the walls and ceiling, various pipes
are exposed. Patches of walls are painted.
Boxes of stuff clutter corners.
Wires hang out of orifices.

Oliver's cottage is bigger, catalogue-smart.

Mike's cottage is small and shit.

There should be birdsong, always,
in the background. And occasionally, planes.

THE VILLAGE BIKE

Punctuation

/
indicates an interrupted line

. . .
indicates the word / line should be protracted

(   )
indicates words which are not heard or not spoken

No punctuation at the end of a line
indicates that the thought is not finished

The layout and position of new lines give
some indication of thought processes and rhythm.
A new line may mean a new thought, or it may
mean the word on the new line took some time
to think of

Act One

ONE

Bakery Cottage. Night time.
John is in bed, reading. Becky is taking off her make-up in the mirror.

Becky I just think it's a shame to live in such a beautiful place and never get to see it. I'm in my car and off to school and why did we even move here if it wasn't to be a bit more
    I don't know
    rustic?

John What did it say?

Becky One lady owner. Hardly ever been ridden. And it's good exercise.

John Yeah . . .

Becky It is. Why do you say it like that?

John I think you're better off with yoga.

Becky It's to get round on. I can still do yoga.

John As well?

Becky I've got to do yoga for my pelvic floor. You don't want me to end up with a bucket do you?

John No.

Becky And this is just to
    you know. They're saying the weather's going to be like this for weeks. A proper heatwave. I don't need to rush anywhere, just make the most of being in the countryside. Clean air. Quiet roads. It'll be good for me.

John OK but let's go into town. Go to the bike shop.

Becky I already called the man.

John Oh.

Becky He seemed really nice. Lives in that barn on Birdleigh Hill.

John That big refurb?

Becky Dunno.

John 'Hunter's Barn'. We looked at a thatch a couple of miles down the road.

Becky Did we? Well anyway he said he could bring it round on Tuesday. It's got those handlebars
   what do you call them?

John I won't be here on Tuesday.

Becky What? Why where will you be?

John I'm going to Amsterdam on Sunday aren't I? Regenerative anti-ageing / whatsit.

Becky I thought that was a week on Sunday.

John It's this Sunday. Can't he come tomorrow?

Becky He can't. I asked. His wife's going away somewhere. What do you call those handlebars?

John Dunno.

Becky Yes you do. Something and / something.

John No idea / what you're talking about.

Becky Like dogs.

John Can't he come when I'm back? I just
   I want to see it.

Becky Awww. No John! I need to start exercising. Look at me!

John Just to be on the safe side.

Becky But it wastes a whole week of holidays! What about if I just get him to bring it? and I look at it? and if I think there's something wrong with it I won't buy it?

John How will you know?

Becky I'll ask the man.

John The man. Is the one selling it.

Becky So what?

John So you don't know where it's been. Who's been on it.

Becky Who's been on it? Why does it / matter who's been on it?

John You know what I mean. I just mean

Becky It's his wife's! His wife's been on it.

John So he says.

Becky I said he's nice. And plus
   we know where he lives. If the bike's shit you can go round his house and sort him out. OK?

John Can't you just wait till I'm back?

Becky I'm running out of time!

John Becky

Becky Fussing!

John I'm not / fussing.

Becky Fussing! What did we say yesterday?

John OK
   OK.

Becky Just –

She puffs air out: 'Let's all calm down.'

John Sorry baby. Sorry.

Becky Stupidface.

John Pinhead.

Becky Dumbass.

They smile at each other.

I bought something else today too.

John Oh yeah?

Becky Want to see?

John Sure.

Becky Don't laugh.

John Why would I laugh?

Becky I have to put it on. Wait there.

She goes into the bathroom.

John Oh I meant to say. Don't forget we're expecting Jenny tomorrow.

Becky Jenny who?

John I knew you'd forget. From the fete. With the husband in the medicine sans frontwhatsit.

Becky Oh God.

She goes into the bathroom. Shuts the door.

John Amazing fellow. They've got two. Both boys I think she said.

Becky (*off*) What?

John We had this great chat about you.

Becky (*off*) I can't really hear you.

John And listen, I know we agreed I'd have a go at the pipes in the morning but she told me about this fantastic organic butchers just out past the White Hart. On a farm. Only they shut at twelve on a Saturday apparently so I thought I might head out there first thing? Pick up the meat for the lasagne? What do you reckon?

Becky opens the door. She is wearing a little white nightie. Strikes an awkward sort of a pose.

Becky (*off*) I didn't hear any of that.

John I said I want to go to the butcher's tomorrow morning but I don't want you to think I'm neglecting the pipes.

Becky I'm
showing you this?

John Oh. Yes. New nightie. Very nice.

Becky What do you think?

Beat.

John Pretty.

Beat.

Where's it from?

Becky laughs.

Becky Where's it from?

John I dunno.

Becky I thought maybe
you know

She climbs on to the bed.

John Oh.

Becky What?

John I've got an early start.

Becky It's not even midnight.

John I've got to make a lasagne tomorrow. From scratch.

Becky John!

John I know, I just

Becky You don't like it.

John I love it. It's great. I'm just
a bit
tired or

Becky Tired?

John hot. Sorry baby. It's just this weather. Are you upset?

Becky No! It's fine. I'm just feeling loads better. And it's the first night of the holidays and I saw this and I thought
but you know. Doesn't matter.

John I love you very much, you know?

Becky I know. I love you too.

John And you're very sexy.

Becky Even now?

John Even now.

They kiss.
She gets into bed.

Actually it's interesting because I was just reading this that Jenny recommended

He waves his book.

and listen to this:
hang on a sec

Becky It's OK.

John no it's interesting. Listen. Ah. Here we go: 'Between the moment you conceive and the day your menstrual cycle resumes you experience hormonal changes that are more dramatic than at any other time in your life including at menopause' blah blah 'yet'

Becky John

John (no wait) 'scientists are only beginning to unravel the impact that this hormonal *rollercoaster* has on the symptoms you experience during pregnancy and on how your brain functions such as pregnancy-related *forgetfulness*
    mood swings' uh huh 'and –'

Becky Piss off.

John wait for it
    '*changes in your libido.*' See?

    He snaps the book shut.

Looks pretty good you know. This plan.

Becky Uh huh?

John It's all like food choices. Getting enough sleep.

Becky I'm already / doing those things.

John How much weight to gain. Exercise? Well you want to do that anyway but this is like integrated into a proper programme to give you the what does he call it? 'The New Pregnancy Ideal'. So the baby turns out perfect. You know what I mean. Not perfect. Just
    OK. Healthy. Normal.

Becky Yeah well. You know. Actually. I don't need it. Because I've made my own programme. And I'm starting it tomorrow. So

John Really? What is it?

Becky Eat peanuts. Drink vodka.

John Very funny.

Becky And ride my new bike. Fast. Down hills.

He looks at her.

I'm doing it
  my way. Right?

John Right.

Becky Thank you.

John But can I just say apparently peanuts are OK now. They changed their minds.

Becky What about vodka?

John Still bad.

Becky You're a good man. Aren't you?

John What makes you say that?

Becky You care. You want to look after me.

John I do.

Becky And I appreciate that.

She snuggles into him. They peck on the lips. She puts her head on his shoulder.

Sure you don't want to
  ?

John Ah yes. You reminded me. So I'll get going on the pipes once I've been to the butcher's. That OK?

Becky How long will that take?

John I dunno. A couple of hours?

Becky Can't you just go to Tesco?

John No! I'm not getting meat from Tesco.

Becky Fine. / Don't start.

John If we all cared a bit more instead of mindlessly trudging round Tesco we wouldn't be in the state we're in.

Becky I said fine! Just don't forget to do the pipes. It's driving me crazy. Waiting for it to happen all the time like

> *Becky listens for a noise.*
> *John yawns.*

on edge in case it starts.

John I know baby, but we're getting there. It just takes time.

Becky OK . . .

John Yeesh!

> *John turns out his bedside lamp.*

Becky Are you going to sleep?

John I thought you wanted to.

> *Becky stares at him.*

What?

Becky Doesn't matter.

John You want to read? I don't mind.

Becky No.

John OK.

> *He kisses her.*
> *Lies down.*
> *She looks at him. Then lies down. Then sits up again straight away.*

Becky Sit-up-and-beg.

John Whah?

Becky The handlebars. You ride like this:

She puts out her arms as if holding on to old-fashioned handlebars.

Up and straight and the wind in your face. Makes you feel
  I don't know
  powerful.

John Uh huh.

Becky gets out of bed. Kneels on the floor.

What are you doing?

She is looking under the bed.

I thought we were going to sleep.

Becky You know I could never ride with no hands when I was a kid. Could you? I'd see boys on their bikes just shooting down the road with their hands by their sides, I thought it was so cool. I could do one hand? And I'd be riding thinking let go let go but it came to that moment and I never could.

She is dragging a cardboard box out from under the bed.

John What are you doing?

Becky I found it earlier. This is meant to be

She reads the marker-pen label written on the side of the box

'Wedding Crockery. Spare.'

She opens the box.

John Why's that under there?

Becky It was in the attic pile.

John Yeah, that's for storage. Don't open it!

Becky I already did. I was looking for a bowl. And guess what I found?

> *She has now opened the box. Inside, DVDs. She picks one up, shows it to him.*

John What's that? I can't see from here.

Becky This one? Or all of them. This one in particular is *Young Sluts Two* did you mean this one or the box in general?

> *Silence.*

Why are you doing your naughty face?

John I'm not. I just it's weird because I didn't think we even brought them with us.

Becky You told me you put them in the bin.

John I did! Someone must have taken them out.

Becky What and bought a load of new ones?

John Maybe one of the removal men or

Becky John!

John What?

Becky One of the removal men did not salvage your porn stash from the rubbish and hide it in the Wedding Crockery Spare box OK? You did. And it's fine! I know why.

John No / I just

Becky But you don't need to worry. OK? In fact I was thinking . . . why don't we watch one?

John What?

Becky Be like the old days. Come on. What about . . .
Get Me Wet Mr Plumber! Or
 Ooh. *The Intruder*. Or . . .
 Wow. *Threesome Addicted Euro Sluts*? This is
definitely new.

John You said you'd gone off it.

Becky No. I said I didn't want it on every time we had
sex.

John I didn't put it on / every time we had sex.

Becky Nearly every time you did. Yes you did.

John This is ridiculous. I'm going to sleep!

 He shuts his eyes.

Becky What was that one with the highwayman? I want
that one.

John Wenches.

Becky Is that here?

John Somewhere.

Becky *Cheating Housewives Three*. John!

 He opens his eyes.

John That's an old one.

Becky 'See this home-wrecking bitch get caught,
punished and covered in cum. This is hardcore at its
best.' Hmm.

John It's actually not that hardcore.

Becky Oh! Here!

 Lifts one out, triumphantly. It is Wenches.

This is more like it, listen to this: 'A world of unquenchable passion is spread before us as well-mannered and virginal Eva travels backwards in time to experience the wild sexual appetites of eighteenth-century England. When she meets Longfellow, the daring Highwayman who kidnaps and ravishes her, he unleashes a wild side which threatens to take over!' Wanna watch it?

We don't have to do anything.

His eyes are closed.

Fine.

She goes to the DVD player. Puts the film in. He opens his eyes.

John You putting it on?

Becky Why not?

He shuts his eyes again. A lull while the DVD loads. Just before she presses 'play':

I just want us to be able to talk about these things. You know? Because if there was
you know a a
fantasy or
something you know that you wanted to
explore then
you know
I hope we could look at that together. Don't you think?

John There isn't.

Becky There might be.

John I'm just saying. There isn't.

Becky OK.

John So.

The pipes bang violently. Becky jumps. Shouts out.
Covers her hands with her ears.

Becky Fuck!
This house is falling apart!

John Calm down!

Becky Don't tell me / to calm down!

John For goodness sake Becky!

Becky What?

> *The noise stops.*
> *Beat.*

John There. Over.

Becky Good.

> *Beat.*

Can we do it tomorrow? You're going away on Sunday.

John Sure. Let me get the meat first and I'll take another look.

Becky I don't mean the pipes! I mean us! I know you're busy just
at some point. Tomorrow.

John Course. OK then. Tomorrow night maybe. Love you.

Becky Love you too.

John Night-night.

> *She presses 'play'. He shuts his eyes.*
> *The porn begins. Exciting classical music. He opens his eyes. He looks at her.*

Becky What?

John Nothing.

He shuts his eyes. Turns over. She watches.

TWO

Bakery Cottage. Evening. The remnants of lasagne on the table.

The pipes are groaning and banging. Jenny, John and Becky are gathered at the back door. Becky has her hands over her ears. She is wearing a short red dress, heels. Dressed to kill.

They wait.

John Any second now.

They wait a bit more. Suddenly, the noise stops.

There.

Jenny God. Any idea what's causing it?

John I'm determined to get to the bottom of it but uh as yet. No joy.

Jenny I know a great plumber. If you need one. Lives in the village.

Becky That could be good.

Jenny If he does still live in the village. I think he does. His wife died a couple of years ago. Childhood sweethearts. Very sad.

John Thanks but I think I'll manage.

Becky It's not a defeat if you call a plumber darling.

John I know!

Becky He doesn't want to admit he can't do it.

John I can do it!

Becky Can you imagine? That noise? Any time of day or night.

John Gives her flashbacks to the old days, doesn't it darling?

Becky John –

John She used to live in a bedsit over a railway station.

Becky John!

John Trains coming and going all night she says she didn't sleep for
    how long were you there sweetheart?

> *Becky looks at him.*

Years though. Wasn't it. Till I came along and rescued her.

> *Jenny prods Becky.*

Jenny You lucky thing.

Becky It was great to meet you!

Jenny Yes! You too! We must do it again now we know where we are. And if there's anything you want to know. Any questions
    problems /
    anything!

Becky Brilliant.

Jenny It's a wonderful
    magical time darling isn't it? But an old veteran like me can be worth her weight in gold. Believe you me. When the old hormones start to whizz round.

John When they *start*?

Becky pokes John.

Becky Darling!

He laughs.

Jenny Wonderful you're so involved though John. I mean not that Jules didn't do his best. But you!

Jenny adopts a gesture of open worship towards John.

There you were. Standing at the bookstall and I'm thinking goodness me. Who's this dashing figure of a man and how and why is his nose buried in a baby book?!

Becky pulls a face of furious frustration. Then covers it, closing her eyes, hanging her head.

John We're just glad to meet a local mum.

Jenny Oh look, poor love. Your wife needs to go to bed John. And I'd better get back before Mother breaks in to the wine cellar.

John I meant to ask you. What happened with your au pair? I told you didn't I darling Jenny was having / some trouble with the au pair?

Becky I think / so. Yes.

Jenny Trouble! Trouble understates it! Ever since the sun came out
well! Skirts up to here. No sign of a bra for love nor money. I kept trying to drop hints but she's Polish and her English is 'not great' so in the end I thought no. I'm just going to have to come straight out with it. I said listen Monika you're in my house and in my house we play by my rules. I've got two young boys. Very impressionable. Not to mention my husband! I didn't say that obviously I said I said I've got two young boys. Very impressionable and I know it's been very hot but I'd appreciate it if you'd find a skirt long enough to at least cover your *knickers*.

Becky And what did she say?

Jenny She said 'I not wearing any knickers.'

Becky No!

John And / was she?

Becky What did you say?

Jenny I said pack your bags right now! She said she was joking. 'Is joke Mrs Leger!' I said too late love. And off she went. Right before the school bloody holidays thanks a bunch!

John Well if you need a hand at all. Becky's on holiday aren't you love?

Becky I mean

John Be good to get some practice in?

Beat.

Jenny Plenty of time for all that isn't there? No and anyway. I'm excited. Gives me a chance to spend more time with them. Sebastian started Latin this term. I think he needs to get out and get muddy. You know? Come here you. Thank you so much for inviting me.

She embraces John.

John Thanks for coming.

John and Jenny kiss cheeks. Becky opens the back door.

Jenny Your lasagne was absolutely delicious. I can't believe you made it from scratch. You're so clever. Isn't he clever?

Becky Yeah.

John Well, it's thanks to your recommendation really.

Jenny I know! I'm so glad you went! Roger's super isn't he?

John You should have seen this place darling. Big fields. Beautiful barns. He said to me 'That cow had the life of Riley. Green grass. Organic food.'

Becky Great.

John You can even take the kids down. Feed the baby animals.

Jenny Gorgeous.

Becky Then can you watch them get slaughtered?

John Becky!

Becky What?

Jenny No you can! Not at Roger's obviously. But my friend Juliet and her husband have started keeping pigs? He's into all that. You know. Making his own cheese and rearing his own bacon. Wonderful actually. And the key is
   apparently
   the children can help rear the pigs
   but you never give the pig a name. So the child doesn't ascribe it with any kind of
   whatdyoumacallums

John Characteristics

Jenny Precisely. Feelings. Or
   whatever. So no one cries when they cut the pig's throat.

Becky John's into this whole supporting local business thing. He puts a lot into it don't you.

   Becky yawns.

ah sorry excuse me, don't you darling?

John Ethical sourcing.

Becky That's the one.

John Because happy meat
  tastes amazing.

Jenny It does. It did! You're a superstar but look John.
Becky's exhausted poor lamb. I really am going now. So
lovely to meet you darling.

Becky Lovely to meet you too.

  They kiss cheeks.

Jenny Oh and good luck with your bicycle! When's it
arriving?

Becky Tuesday.

Jenny Lovely. Well you must bring it round. Give me a
demonstration. And don't let Oliver Hardcastle give you
any grief!

John Who's that?

Becky Bike man.

Jenny Very odd man.

Becky He was nice on the phone.

John What do you mean 'odd'?

Becky I'm sure he's fine.

Jenny No course he's fine. Sorry I'm not
  he's not a serial killer or anything! Just
  you know. Not my cup of tea.

Becky He's literally just bringing the bike over. So

Jenny Oh! I completely forgot! I've been meaning to say
to you I've got a load of baby stuff in the attic if you're
interested?

John Oh.

Becky Really?

Jenny Tons of it.

John That'd be great! If you're sure?

Jenny Oh God. Absolutely. It's sitting there taking up space. I keep nagging Jules to get rid of it but he's never here long enough so I'll just bring it over shall I?

John Definitely!

Jenny Great! Well then. I'll give you a call.

John Perfect. Thanks Jenny.

Jenny No thank you. Really. You're such a gorgeous couple. What a gorgeous couple!

John Thanks!

Becky Thanks! Bye-bye!

Jenny Bye kids!

John Bye Jenny!

Becky Bye!

Jenny departs.

Jenny (*off*) Byeeeeeeeeeeeeeee!

Jenny is gone.
    Becky waits a beat. Flicks the back door shut. Lets out a sort of whoop. Turns back to John.
    A moment.

John You OK?

He heads to the washing up.

Becky That was intense.

John She's nice isn't she? And you're a very lucky woman.

Becky Yes. I. am.

She moves towards him.

John Made a lasagne. And now: washing up! What more could you ask for?

Becky Leave that if you want.

John I don't mind.

Becky I'll do it in the morning.

John Won't take long.

Becky Don't you want to go to bed?

John You go baby, if you're tired. I'll be up in a bit.

Becky I mean
together.

Beat.

John Just if you leave it it gets all
you know it's harder to clean off.

Becky looks at him.

I'm a bit full. You go on up. I won't be long.

*He puts the stereo on. Talking. Becky waits a beat.
Then heads up the stairs.*

Becky I might watch another one of your films then if that's OK.

John What's that?

Becky Put another one of those films on.

John Oh. OK.

Becky Yeah. So just
take your time.

Beat.

And don't even bother saying anything about the bike man coming. OK? I don't give a fuck if he is a serial killer. I'm getting that fucking bike. Right?
   Right?

John Right.

Becky Good.

She goes.
   He watches her, a bit confused. Gets on with the washing up.
   Upstairs, Becky takes a DVD and puts it in the machine. It is Get Me Wet Mr Plumber. *Becky watches it and wanks.*

THREE

Bakery cottage. Morning.
   In the kitchen, Mike is holding a spanner. Becky is in her dressing gown. They are staring up at a drip coming from a pipe. The drip drips into a bucket.

Becky I had visions of the whole house filling up with water. Well you saw. My nightie got soaked. Not that you saw my nightie I mean you saw when it was all
   I just mean I didn't know what to do so
   thanks for
   coming.

   Beat.

Mike You got sweaty pipes. So see. Here –

Becky Uh huh. / Oh yes.

Mike I got to replace it only I haven't got the right part. Thought I had it in the van but I can't find it so

sweaty just means ah
   moist you know because it's like sweat. Dripping and
that.

Becky Right.

Mike It's nice and tight for now but I'll need to pop back /
and

Becky And that
   what you think that'll just

Mike Should drip through. Eventually. Just need to keep
an eye on it till we get the part.

Becky You're my hero! Thank you! Sod's law isn't it?
Alone in the house. Husband away and it chooses today
to start bloody

   He is gazing at her.

shooting
   stuff all over the
      whatsit are you hot? Is it me or is it really hot in here?
I'm burning up!

Mike Record heat. So they say.

   Becky wants to take her dressing gown off but can't.

Becky You're not wrong! Wooh!

   *She fans herself. He smiles. She smiles. They both look
   away at the pipe.*

Mike That noise you mentioned?

Becky Oh yes? You think it could be connected?

Mike Could be.

Becky One thing leads to another. Sort of thing. Is it?

   Beat.

Mike What's above here? Bathroom is it?

Becky I think it's the uh bedroom. Do you need to take a look?

Mike Depends what you want me to do.

Becky I mean

He checks the time.

I don't want to do anything behind my husband's I mean just the plumbing's kind of his 'area' so what about tea? Can I make you a cup of tea? Is that? Normal?

He smiles at her. Laughs a little.

Mike Cup of tea wouldn't go astray.

Becky Great. Great! How do you take it? Your tea.

Mike Milk two sugars. Thanks.
       Thanks a lot.

He gazes at her. She turns away to boil the kettle.

Becky I used to live in flats. You know? Before I met my husband. I never owned anywhere so it was like oh there's a problem. Call the landlord. You know? This is the first time I've ever
       and you hear these terrible stories don't you?

Mike You do.

Becky But turns out if you need something done. You can pay a man. And he just
       comes in and does it!

Beat.

Mike Where's he gone then? Your husband?

She crosses her arms.

Becky Um. Amsterdam?

Mike Oh yeah?

Becky He's filming a skin-cream commercial.

Mike That what he told you?

He laughs. Becky laughs too, out of politeness.

No that's good. Will I see it on the telly?

Becky Hopefully.

Mike I'll look out for it.

Beat.

Becky I'm pregnant!

Mike Oh!

Becky I know. You can't tell.

Mike Congratulations.

Becky Yeah you know. Thanks.

The doorbell goes.

Saved by the bell. I mean. Sorry. Will you excuse me?
Two seconds

She exits.
  Mike looks at the bucket. It's his and he wants to take it back. He picks it up. Looks for something to replace it with. But he can't find anything and meanwhile the drip is going on the floor.
  The kettle boils.
  Oliver enters. He is dressed as a highwayman. Carrying a bicycle.
  Mike shoves the bucket back under the drip.

Oliver About to do my 'stand and *deliver*' and I think fuck! The bike!

Becky follows him in. She seems a little flustered.

36

Becky You're OK. I wasn't busy.

Oliver No well. I can see that. Eleven o'clock in the morning and you're still not dressed!

Becky Oh.

Oliver Oh hi sorry is this your

Becky Oh

Oliver Oh Mike! Sorry, I didn't see you there. Oliver Hardcastle you did my sewage pump last year.

Mike Course I did. Sorry, mate. How are you?

Oliver Yeah you know. Same old. And you?

Becky Mike's having a look at our pipes.

Mike Sweating.

Oliver Oh no.

Becky I'm
    on holiday. And water started coming out and I had to call Mike and
    usually I'd be up I just

Oliver Where shall I stick her?

Becky Maybe

Oliver Stick her here for the moment.

Becky Thanks.

> *During the following, Mike cleans up his tools.*
> *Checks the pipe again. Fills out an invoice form for*
> *the job.*

Oliver Now. Something I need to say to you. I didn't realise when we spoke but there is a small hitch. I took her for a test ride
    last night

just down the hill from the barn, make sure everything was OK

and I was halfway down and the chain came off. Now I've put it back on for the moment but

Becky Oh I see.

Oliver No it's totally fine I was probably just riding her a bit hard. She needs a bit of tinkering. Maybe get your husband to have a go.

Becky OK it's just no it's great it's just he's away so

Oliver Oh.

Becky and I've been waiting but

Oliver You can still ride her?

Becky Better not.

Oliver No, just don't go too fast.

Becky It's OK. I still want it.

Oliver OK well. Take her for now but let me know if you've got any problems.

Becky Would you like a cup of tea or / do you have to get back?

Oliver I should probably get back.

Becky Yes.

Oliver Though to be fair they could do the scenes where I'm dead.

Becky I'm making one anyway.

She clicks the kettle back on to boil.

Oliver Stabbed through the heart with a rapier. Or in this case

a plastic cutlass from a dressing-up box.

38

Becky Oh no.

Oliver Well. I have my fun before I go. Killing. Robbery. Bit of ravishing.

Becky Who do you kill?

Oliver Mainly people in carriages. For their jewels. But in the end Lord Egghart tries to force my lady love into an arranged marriage. I fly into a jealous rage. Fight a duel. Kill the lord and then get set upon by an angry mob!

Becky Poor you!

Oliver Are you a student?

Becky No.

Oliver You said you were on holiday.

Becky I'm an English teacher.

Oliver Ah well all I was going to say is you must come down!

Becky Oh yes! I'd love to!

Oliver And you Mike. You should come along. We don't see you out and about much.

Mike Yeah?

Becky Sounds great.

Oliver Birdleigh Village Hall.

Mike OK.

Oliver Bring a book.

> *He laughs.*
> *The kettle boils again.*

Becky Boiled so uh
white two sugars?

Mike Ta, love.

Becky busies herself with the tea.

How's the missus? Alice is it?

Oliver Alice it is. Off on one of her jaunties. Again. Costs an arm and a leg but there you go. Least I got a month of peace and quiet.

He laughs.

You're a lucky man Mike. Living out there on your own. I envy you.

Becky Did you want tea?

Oliver Best not. I'll head off in a minute. Just catching my breath.

Becky Do you want to sit down?

Oliver I'd love to sweetheart but my britches are somewhat
    restrictive. I'm pretty sure
    don't quote me on this but I'm pretty sure Jean arranges it with costume to make sure they're extra tight.

Becky Ha. Oh! Well they look – very nice so

Oliver People in this village. You gotta watch em.

Mike Jean Mundy this is?

Oliver She insists we're in costume all through rehearsals to help us 'get into the roles'. Because you're never too old for a fetish. Are you Mike?

Mike Oh well. I wouldn't know about all that.

Becky laughs, a bit. Gets on with making tea.
    Oliver and Mike look at the bike.

She's a pretty one though.

Oliver Isn't she gorgeous?

Becky turns her head, sharp. Worried they were talking about her.

Hardly been ridden. Got Alice one of those new Minis
for Christmas and the bike's been in the garage ever since
just
    gathering dust. She was expensive.

Mike Looks it.

Oliver watches Becky as she carries the tea.

Becky Your tea Mike. Oh!

She spills some, her hand is shaking.

Oliver You OK there?

Becky Sorry. I'll get a cloth.

Mike Ta love. Tell you what. I can have a look at this for
you if you like.

Becky Oh no.

Mike I don't mind. It's only the chain.

Oliver Well. No, it's my responsibility I should do it
really just
    my costume.

Becky And anyway I've got to go out in a bit.

Oliver Tell you what. When's your husband back?

Becky Tomorrow. Night.

Oliver I'll come back in the morning.

Becky Oh. I mean

Oliver I insist.

Becky If you could that would be brilliant.

Oliver My wife would kill me if anything happened. What sort of time? Is early OK?

Becky Early's fine but what about the money?

Oliver I'll come early then. Oh I don't know. Money money. Just
pay me after.

He smiles. They look at each other just a beat too long. She nods. Then:

Well! I'd best be off or I'll have Jean on my case.

Becky I'll see you out.

Oliver See you, Mike. / Nice to see you again.

Mike Right you are. Yeah. Good luck with it.

Becky and Oliver leave.
Mike looks quickly round the kitchen. He goes to a cupboard, high up. Opens it. Loads of Tesco bags ping out. He stuffs them hurriedly back in. Looks in another cupboard. Gives up.
Becky comes back in. She has a strange expression on her face.

Mike You OK love?

Becky I'm fine thanks. How are you?

Beat.

Mike You got a bucket?
Or a saucepan / or

Becky Oh. / Sorry.

Mike Sorry it's just

Becky I'll get a pan.

Mike I always say if you find something good. You got to keep hold of it.

Becky fetches a saucepan from a cupboard.

My nephew. Lives in town. Always on at me to get a new van. He says your van Uncle Mike is the public face of your business. And he's probably right. You know? She's all knacked out and rusty. But I got memories in that van. I call her Elsie. Don't ask me why. Came to me one day. Can't send Elsie to the scrapyard. Break my heart.

She hands him the pan. He swaps it for the bucket.

You just get attached to things don't you? Or I do. Thanks Becky.

She looks at him. Slightly affronted. Then smiles.

Becky No worries.

He hugs the bucket to him.

Mike Your uh invoice is on the table there. I didn't have the part so I'm just charging you the standard call-out fee. Seventy.

Becky Is a cheque OK?

Mike Cheque is perfect.

Becky Excellent. Hang on a sec.

She goes to a drawer.

Just grab my
   and find a
   here's a pen. Now where's my
   chequebook's usually in here so uh

She rummages in the drawer. Slams it shut. Mike jumps.

I think my husband's moving things again. Sorry about this!

She flings open some other drawers, bangs them shut.

43

Mike cowers.

Check my handbag sorry Mike hold on a second.

She goes to her handbag.

Mike No rush.

She is searching.

Take your time.

It's not in her bag.

Becky Shit. SHIT. I can't find it. Is there
I don't have any cash.

Mike Ah.

She is a bit out of breath from her frantic searching.

Becky You don't have a machine or
No sorry I'm not really used to uh
what can we do? Is there something we can do?

Mike Like

Becky I mean

Beat.

Mike You could post it?

Becky Post it! Yes! Brilliant.

Mike My address is on the / invoice there.

Becky OK. Oh yes. I'll find it and post you a cheque.
Sorry about that.

Mike No worries. He's a funny chap isn't he?

Becky Sorry?

Mike What my wife would have called 'eccentric'.

Becky smiles.

FOUR

Bakery Cottage. Late evening.

Porn-type music comes from the laptop. Becky is watching, drinking wine. The light from the screen flickers over her face. On the kitchen table, an open bottle of wine.

The water from the pipe drips into the saucepan. Jenny arrives through the back door.

Jenny Halloo? Are you decent?

Becky Is that you?

Jenny hustles in, with baby things. Becky quickly shuts the computer, just remembers to put the wine glass down and heads downstairs.

It is you. Come in. Come in. Ooh!

Jenny This is just the start of it!

Becky Right! Oh great. Wow . . .

Jenny For some reason couldn't find the bouncer.

Becky Oh no don't be silly.

Jenny I hope you don't mind only when you said pop over I thought may as well 'kill two birds with one stone'.

Becky No, that's brilliant. John's going to be
   wow.

Jenny Oh John! What a hero. I was thinking that on my way over. I know he's left you for a few days but it's manageable isn't it? A few days at a time. Is here OK?

Becky Thanks. Perfect.

Jenny Poor Jules is 'stuck in El Salvador'. Again. Oh look! It's Bunny!

She jangles a baby rabbit with bells on.

You used to be favourite didn't you Bunny? And now what? Does nobody love you? Does nobody want you?

Becky Do you want some wine?

Jenny Are you drinking?

Becky I was just going to have the one.

Jenny I'll have one but really darling don't on my account. Now wait. This might cheer you up. Look what else I've brought . . .

She chucks Bunny down. Reaches into her handbag.

Wait for it –

Produces a massive block of chocolate.

Ta-da! You can't have an emotional crisis without chocolate can you? Let's eat it quick before it melts!

Becky Aw thanks Jenny. Thanks for coming round. I really appreciate it.

Jenny shuts the back door. Becky gets two fresh glasses.

Jenny Not at all it's my pleasure. Mum owes me a night off anyway. You should really keep this door locked you know. When John's away.

Becky is pouring them wine.

Seventy-two hours on my own with the boys I'm either going to drop dead of exhaustion or
    I don't know what. Please just talk to me like a human. Come on. Out with it. What's up?

46

Becky Oh. Well. It's nothing big. It's just

Jenny notices the bicycle.

Jenny The bike! It came!

Becky Yeah. Um, thingy brought it round. Oliver. It's kind of
what I wanted to talk to you about.

Jenny Uh-oh. What did he do?

Becky No! No it's nothing like that. It's more like
something to do with my body. Which happened.
Earlier. And I can't tell if it's a baby thing or more

Jenny A physical symptom?

Becky Kind of. It's a bit –

Jenny Trust me darling. Once you've been through
childbirth you completely lose all sense of shame. You
sit with your legs open in a room full of strangers all
staring at your thingumadoodle. Nothing you can say
will shock me.

Becky OK. It's just that me and John
since I got pregnant

Jenny Cheers.

Becky Cheers. In the bedroom. We haven't really – 'done
it'. And it's creating quite a lot of um stress?

Jenny Uh huh. Oh isn't this wonderful? I can't tell you
how wonderful this is after three days of Bob the Builder.
Sorry darling. Carry on.

Becky I just don't know what to do. Because it's like if
your body is literally telling you what it needs. More than
ever before

Jenny You're very in tune with it.

Becky exactly yes and at the same time there's him. And he's wanting the complete opposite. Do you know what I mean?

Jenny I think it's pretty normal.

Becky Really?

Jenny yawns.

Jenny Ah it just changes things. Doesn't it?

Becky Yes! But this is what I say. I say he's being different. And he says I'm being different.

Jenny You are different! He surely can't expect you to stay the same?

Becky No. I don't know.

Jenny Darling put it this way. It's a bloody miracle we even had Nathaniel. To be honest as soon as I had Seb I just
    God it sounds awful doesn't it but I just you know down there's all
    eeh and not because of Jules. I still found him 'attractive' I just had no desire to

Becky Oh.

Jenny And then since Nate
    well you're just so tired. All the time. I think it's normal. You've got other things to think about haven't you? We're not like them. Thinking about it every five seconds of the day! Though I probably get off light compared to you. Jules is away so much I really never have to do much fending off these days!

Becky But if you don't
    I mean if you two don't ever
    you don't think he might
    do anything?

Jenny You mean

Becky With someone else I mean.

Jenny Oh I see. I mean
    God. You don't know you do? I know he had a crush. Once. There was an aid nurse. Anna. Italian or

Becky And what happened?

Jenny I can't remember now. I think she got engaged to a major. Oh God. Darling. John's not –

Becky No! God no. No. He's over the moon about the baby.

Jenny Because it's a funny time isn't it? I think some men go a bit

Becky Do you think?

Jenny Wife-beating. For example. Very common during pregnancy. Not that John's likely to

Becky laughs.

is he?

Becky No!

Jenny No but they can get funny about s-e-x. Too. Remember what happened to Sally Montgomery?

Becky No.

Jenny When she was having her third. Oh course you weren't here then. Sorry darling. I'm going a bit wazoo. But anyway yes. When all those prostitutes got done in, her husband was interviewed. Turned out he'd been down there picking up 'whores'. Had to give a statement to police.

Becky Did they think it was him?

Jenny No no. God no he just might have seen something.

Becky And had he?

Jenny No I just mean the embarrassment. One of them was only sixteen apparently.

Becky Oh no.

Jenny Sally was chair of the PTA at St Michael's. She had to stand down.

Becky *She* did?

Jenny I don't know if she *had* to but she did. They moved actually.

Becky No but

Jenny To Leamington Spa.

Becky What I mean is
I mean
what happens to me?

Jenny When?

Becky Now. Next. It's like
before
I knew who I was. And now
who am I?

Jenny You're having an identity crisis.

Becky No. I just mean
is that what they want? Tight
pussies?

Jenny What?!

Becky I feel like I'm losing something.

Jenny You mean
giving birth is going to

50

Becky No! I don't just mean that. Or maybe I do. I mean. They. Have all the power.

Jenny Men?

Becky No! Them. The nurse. Your nanny with the short skirt.

Jenny Monika?

Becky That's why you got rid of her. Isn't it?

Jenny I'm a bit lost darling. Start again. I'm not with you.

Becky I called that plumber today.

Jenny Mike? He's not responsible for this is he?

She means the drip.

Becky No no. He was great. / It's just

Jenny Oh good.

Becky How do I say it? I feel
  safe. Not safe that's the wrong word because I don't feel safe with the plumber I feel the opposite of safe but I feel like
  when he looks at me

Jenny The plumber?

Becky Yes! When he looks at me. I know he wants to have sex with me.

Jenny Mike?!

Becky Yes.

Jenny Mike the plumber? Mike the plumber wants to have sex with you? What makes you say that?

Becky Because of the way he looks at me.

Jenny You know his wife died of cancer.

Becky What's that got to do with it?

Jenny I'm just saying.

Becky It's not the point.

Jenny He might be lonely.

Becky That's not what I'm saying! I'm not saying he's in love with me, I'm saying
   not even he *wants* to have sex with me I just mean he *would*.

Jenny Based on what?

Becky Based on his eyes. You must know what I'm talking about. I'm talking about men and how most of them would probably have sex with you if you gave them a chance. You know.

Jenny With me?

Becky With me. That's how I deal with
   men. I assume
   they want to have sex with me.

Jenny How complex.

Becky I haven't explained.

Jenny You poor thing. You know all this it's so

   Becky reaches for the wine bottle.

leave that maybe

   Jenny swipes the wine out the way.

so normal. Everything you're talking about. Of course you're scared and
   anxious and all that stuff and your body's changing and your hormones are going crazy but believe me darling once it's born? You won't give two hoots about any of this. I promise you. When you hold that little baby

you'll love it so much
   you won't care about anything else.
   Don't look like that. It's a good thing! It's liberating!
And look in the meantime
   you've got the whole summer. You can take things
easy. Get out on your nice new bike! Carefully of course.
Nice and slow.

   They look at the bike.

Becky It's broken.

Jenny Oh!

Becky No it's fine he's
   he said he's coming back to fix it. Didn't I say?

Jenny I don't think so. Did you? Are you OK darling?
You look strange.

Becky I'm fine. No. I'm just
   excited.

FIVE

Bakery Cottage. Early next morning.
   *Becky is in her dressing gown, making tea. Oliver is
sitting by the bike, having a tinker. He is in his normal
clothes. The water from the pipe drips into a saucepan.*

Becky I just think it's such a shame to live somewhere so
beautiful and never see it. I still don't really know my way
round. Have you lived here long?

Oliver About eight years? My wife was born here. Near
enough. The air in other places doesn't agree with her
fragile constitution apparently. So we had to move back.

Becky And you like it?

Oliver I don't mind it. Quiet. Bit small. Bit small . . . minded. You know? The uproar when they opened that Tesco. We had petitions. I think Alice went on a march. Round the village green. Placards. A loudhailer.

Becky John hates Tesco.

Oliver You think there are people out there
  starving

Becky I have to hide the bags. If I've been. I've got a whole stash of them in a cupboard!

Oliver Good for you. Just what a marriage needs. A bit of mystery.

Becky I mean

Oliver Look at your face. I'm joking.

Becky Oh!

  He laughs. Then, she laughs too. He gets back to the bike.

And
  have you got kids or

Oliver Shhh!

Becky Sorry?

Oliver Sore point.

Becky Sorry.

Oliver Not for me. I've got a couple with the first wife and as far as I'm concerned that's me done but Alice wants one of her own and when Alice wants something

  He laughs.

I think I could probably reasonably call it Hysteria. Tick tick tick. 'My eggs! My eggs!' And I don't know about

54

other men but I find sexual intercourse to be more enjoyable when one doesn't feel like a tool being implemented for the sole purpose of impregnation. What about you?

Becky Me?

Oliver No kids?

Becky No! No I mean John wants them. And all our friends have got them so yeah you know I mean I guess soon. We will but
no I don't think sex should be
like that I mean
the opposite. I suppose.

Oliver The opposite?

Becky Not a means to an end. A
just a means or
what do I mean?

Oliver I know what you mean.

Becky Fun. I mean.

Oliver Pleasurable.

Becky Yes.

Oliver The carnal coming together of consenting adults.

Becky Your tea!

Oliver Thanks, just stick it on the table.

Beat.

How you finding it then? Village life? Must make a change from the big smoke?

Becky That's the aim.

Oliver Is that where you met your husband?

Becky In a pub.

Oliver Love at first sight?

Becky Kind of.

Oliver Lust at first sight?

Becky We were at the bar. He looked at me. I looked at him. He explained to me how a beer pump works. Three weeks later I moved in with him.

Oliver How does a beer pump work? I must remember that one.

Becky No I know. It sounds a bit – but it was actually really amazing. John was the one who said I could be a teacher. Never thought I'd be anything. Really. Before I met him. I really love him. He's great.

Oliver You're funny.

    Beat.

Becky Anyway. What was the question? Village life! Yes. No. It's OK! I like it! We've just been so busy since we got here I haven't really had much chance to appreciate it.

Oliver 'Doing the house'?

Becky Ha.

Oliver People love all that don't they? 'Doing the house'.

Becky Do they?

Oliver Bet you watch the telly programmes and everything don't you? House porn.

Becky No.

Oliver Course you do.

Becky I prefer real porn.

Oliver Do you?

Becky No!

Oliver Do you?

Becky If I did I wouldn't tell you.

Oliver You just did.

Becky I just said it to shut you up.

Oliver You're putting pictures in my mind.

Becky Stop it! It's too hot for this!

Oliver Is it? Is it hot? Is there a heatwave? Do you know what? I would never have known.

He laughs.

People all out there in their shorts on the village green. I saw Pat's wife Jackie the other day in a bikini I thought my eyes were going to shrivel up and fall out my head. Should be illegal if you ask me. Fat old women in bikinis. Or. Actually. Just fat old women. Don't you think?

Beat.

Have I offended you?

Becky No.

Oliver You look offended. You are aren't you? Aw. I'm only teasing. I'm sure you look lovely in a bikini.

Becky I don't think that's the point.

Oliver Bet you do though.

Becky This conversation is
I don't think

Oliver Sorry. Sorry. I'm only winding you up. Force of habit. I apologise. I'll shut up and get on with my job.

Suddenly he catches himself on the bike somehow. He cries out angrily, in pain. Becky jumps.

Fuck!

He grabs the bike, smashes it into the wall. A quick, hard movement which came out of nowhere and is over before there is time to stop it.

It bit me!

Becky What happened?

Oliver Dunno. Fuck!

He holds his finger.

Becky Are you OK?

Oliver Ow.

Becky Show me?

Oliver Nah. It's fine. Bit of blood. I'll live.

He sucks his finger.

Becky Do you need a plaster? I've got plasters here somewhere.

She starts to look around for the plasters.

Oliver Just some wet kitchen towel or something. If you've got it.

Becky Sure. Sorry about that. I feel responsible.

Oliver Do you?

Becky I don't know.

Oliver OK then. It's your fault.

She has got the wet tissue.

Becky Here.

She takes it over to him.

Let me see.

    Oliver holds out his hand. His finger is bleeding quite a lot.

It's deep!

Oliver Is it?

Becky You might need a stitch.

    He tuts.

Oliver Come on.

    She holds his hand. She dabs the tissue on it. The tissue turns red. He watches her tend to his finger. She does not look at him.
    Her breathing changes.
    He watches her.

Becky You need a plaster. Let me get you one.

    Becky steps away from Oliver. Bangs back into the table.

Oliver Mind out.

    Becky hurries upstairs and into the bedroom. Suddenly, the pipes groan and bang. Oliver looks around, alarmed.

What the fuck?

    Upstairs, Becky clambers onto the bed.

What is that?

    She gets on all fours.

Becky Oh god.

    She pants like a dog

Oliver What did you say?

She gets up. Hurries back down the stairs. Stands looking at him.

Becky Don't say anything.

Oliver What?

Becky I SAID DON'T SAY

The pipes stop.

ANYTHING. Sorry.

Oliver What was that?

Becky I need to say something. It's the pipes.

Oliver Where's my plaster?

Becky Stay there. You have to wait.

Oliver Why?

Becky Because I need to say something! Let me say something! I'm going to say something.

She is moving towards him.

Oliver Go on then.

She stands in front of him.

What do you want to say?

Becky I want to say . . .
I want to say . . .
I just want to say

*She touches his chest. Her breathing changes. He doesn't move. She touches his face. She makes a noise like an animal. A small cry, exactly half way between pain and pleasure. And suddenly they are kissing.
Then just as suddenly she is pulling away.*

OK OK OK stop stop / stop stop

Oliver I don't want to stop.

Becky You have to stop. Stop!

He stops.

Stop.

Oliver I've stopped.

Becky You have to go.

Oliver I don't want to.

Becky I don't want you to but you have to. I don't do things like this. It's not me. OK?

Oliver Who is it?

Becky I don't know. It's just
not me. I love my husband.

Oliver I won't tell.

Becky No! It's not the point. I don't
I don't want to.

Beat.

Could you maybe please go now? Please.

He shrugs.
Goes to the door. Pauses.

Oliver Haven't you forgotten something?

Becky Have I?

Oliver My money.

Becky Oh God.

Oliver It's OK.

Becky I'm so sorry. Of course. I'm just
all over the place I don't know what's wrong with me.

I got it ready. Here. Sorry.

She has the money ready in the drawer.

Oliver Thanks.

Becky I'm so sorry.

She hands him the money.

Oliver No problem.

Becky I just

Oliver Listen. If you change your mind

Becky I can't.

Oliver But if you change your mind. Just give me a call.

Music plays. The introduction to the Andy Williams classic, 'Love Story', dramatic, romantic, orchestral. Into:

SIX

Bakery Cottage. Night time. John's luggage scattered around the kitchen.

John is standing at the sink, filling a vase of red roses with water. 'Love Story' now plays on the stereo. John sings along. His voice is loud, surprisingly tuneful.

Becky comes in from the garden, in her nightie. She is barefoot. Her feet are dirty. She has been watering the plants. Now she busies herself in the kitchen. He tries to grab her, she evades him. Turns the music off.

John Oh. I was enjoying that.

Becky You going to take your stuff up?

John You OK my love? Yes. Just doing this.

Becky Is it urgent?

John I want to make it nice for you. What's the grass like?

Becky I don't know. Dry?

John I don't know how Jenny's husband does it you know. They've got two kids. A paddling pool. A climbing frame. And his lawn still looks like centre court at Wimbledon. Are you OK?

Becky Think I'm having a hot flush.

John Possible. It's your body reacting / to the fluctuating hormone levels.

Becky Not now John. Please.

John Hot flushes can / be quite common

Becky John?

John Yes?

Becky I don't want to talk about babies.

John OK.

Beat.

Do you want your surprise now?

Becky You got me a surprise?

John Maybe.

Becky What is it?

John It's a surprise!

Becky You haven't got me a surprise for ages.

John I know. That's what I thought. So I thought I should bring you one now. Here.

He fetches his bag.

Becky Is it a bag of the finest Dutch skunk?

John Ha. What?

Becky Is it . . .

John Hang on a sec.

Becky something you got from duty-free? Perfume? Whisky?

John Perfume can cause infertility in the unborn child.

Becky Five million B&H?

John Here!

He produces a cardboard box.

Perk of the job. Open it.

She takes out a tub of anti-ageing cream. And another. It is a box full of them.

The lady said I could take them. They're really expensive to buy and apparently they're the best on the market. I tried some. I felt really
rejuvenated.

Beat.

Smell it. It smells really nice.

Becky Do you think I look old?

John Don't be silly! Smell it.

Becky I don't want to smell it.

John Actually if anything I think you look younger. It's filled out your cheeks or something.

Becky My cheeks?

John In a nice way. You look divine. Like an earth mother. A goddess. I just thought at some point you might want it. And it was free so

64

Becky Yeah.

John You know I think I missed you more this weekend than I've ever missed you before.

He gazes at her.

You
   are my true love.

Becky I'm too hot.

She gets up.

There's no air.

John Look at you.

Becky What?

John I don't know. You just look so . . .

Becky Stop looking at me like that.

John Like what?

Becky Like something in the zoo.

John What?!

Becky A cage at the zoo.

John Come on. Sit down. Can I get you a drink of something?

Becky Yes. I'll have a vodka tonic.

John Ah. No vodka for mummies.

Becky One vodka is not going to kill it.

John When did you ever have one vodka?

Becky What the fuck is that supposed to mean??

John Calm down! I'm teasing! That was a long time ago.

65

Becky You're not funny. OK? In fact you're fucking annoying.

John OK.

Becky OK?

John OK.

Becky What's that mean? OK?

John It means according to my book the best thing I can do to maintain harmony is indulge your 'needs', agree with you and try to make life better in whatever way I can. Now: would you like a foot rub?

Becky No.

John Head massage?

Becky Go down on me.

John What?

Becky Make me come. With your tongue.

John The book doesn't mention that.

Becky Really?

John I'll run you a bath, no? Put some stuff in.

Becky I don't want a bath.

John A Horlicks?

Becky John.

John Sweetheart

Becky What?

John I've been on a plane.

Becky What about my 'needs'?

John Baby

66

Becky I'm not wearing any knickers.

   Beat.

We've never done it in here.

John You're being weird.

   She moves towards him. He backs away.

I don't like this.

Becky Why not?

John Because I don't
feel like it.

Becky You'd rub my feet.

John It's completely different.

Becky WHY? / Don't shout

John Don't

Becky you'll upset Babooney! Couldn't get enough of me
before could you? When you wanted to conceive your
child. And now it's like you've had your dick chopped off.

John I don't know what you're talking about but I do
know you're very tired and very hormonal / and

Becky And I know you're a complete cunt.

John OK.

Becky I think you've been in Amsterdam fucking
prostitutes!

John What?! OK.

Becky Not going to deny it?

John I don't think I need to deny it because it's ridiculous.

Becky Go down on me then.

John I don't want to.

Becky All shagged out?

John No!

Becky Why not then? Say it. You don't fancy me any more. You think I'm old and fat and disgusting.

John You're crazy! Why are you saying those things? Course I fancy you. I just

Becky WHAT?

John I don't want to kill the baby!
  OK?

  Beat.

Becky You what?

John Our baby's in there.

Becky So?

John What if it's a girl? What if it's a *boy*?!

Becky John. It's in my womb. Not my vagina!

John For God's sake, Becky. I know where the baby is. OK?

Becky But what? What are you talking about?

John I'm talking about my instinct. Right? And my instinct says no. We can go a few months without sex can't we?

Becky No!

John Course we can! Stop being a
  –

Becky A what?

John This is so unfair. I'm not just a
  piece of meat Becky. I'm your husband.

Becky I don't give a fuck who you are.

John You're scaring me.

Becky Please John. Please?

John No!

Becky Oh God.

She starts crying.

John Becky love. Listen. Come here.

She goes over to him. He puts his arms around her and pulls her to him. Comforts.

There we go.

She wipes her nose on his shoulder. She kisses him. He moves his head away. She kisses him again. They kiss for a bit. She tries to push him against the wall. She reaches for his crotch. Undoes his fly. He wriggles about a bit. Fiddles with it himself. Jiggles up and down.

Becky Are you

John Hang on a sec

Becky Is it

John It's not

Becky Is it not

She feels his crotch. He is not hard. They stay like that for a moment. She steps away. Freezes. He watches her.

John I can
do things
anyway.

Becky Wow. Thanks.

John I don't
mind?

Becky You wouldn't enjoy it.

John I might.

Becky You wouldn't. Trust me. I've done it loads of times when I didn't really want to.

Beat.

It's shit.

He laughs. A bit.

John Not with me!

Becky What? Yes with you. Course with you. That's what I'm saying. Don't do it. It's horrible. It makes you feel like shit.

SEVEN

Bakery Cottage. Night time. A slant of moonlight falls on John, snoring in bed.

Downstairs in the kitchen, Becky stares into a laptop. The blue flickering lights her face. She is watching porn on the internet. She is clicking furiously between images. She finds something. Reaches in between her legs. Then suddenly, changes her mind.

She stands up. Gets her phone. Presses buttons. A moment.

Another moment.

Becky Oh hi. Sorry to call so late. It's uh Becky? The um you sold me your bicycle. I just wondered if you'd be about. Soon. Maybe we could I don't know.
Hang out?

End of Act One.

Act Two

ONE

Birdleigh Hill. Morning.
   Becky is on her bike, with music on her headphones, a floaty dress not perfect for cycling. She pedals hard. She lets go with one hand, wobbles. The hill steepens. She grabs hold with both hands. Lifts up out of the saddle and pedals standing.

TWO

Hunter's Barn. Afternoon. Dust in the air.
   Oliver holds two cups of tea. He is wearing tracksuit trousers. No top. Maybe he has an old tattoo somewhere.

Oliver I'm glad the bike held out up the hill.

   Beat.

Nice to see her getting some use. Scrubs up well doesn't she?

   Becky emerges from the bathroom. She is wearing her floaty dress.

Becky What time is it?

Oliver It's
   just after four.

Becky Wow.

Oliver Teatime.

Becky Thank you.

Oliver My pleasure.

Becky Your house is nothing like I imagined.

Oliver Ah well. Alice is in charge of the decorating.

Becky Didn't think you'd be so
dunno
House and Garden.

Oliver Should I be flattered or offended?

Becky I don't know.

Oliver I like things tidy. What can I say?

Becky Lucky you. Our house is a bomb site. Now we've got all this fucking baby stuff in our spare room. It's a nightmare.

Oliver Baby stuff? Why?

Becky Oh
just
because my husband's obsessed with babies.

Oliver Christ I thought Alice was bad. At least she hasn't bought baby stuff. Bit mental is he?

Becky I think he just
it was a bargain so anyway

She kisses him.

I had a really nice time.

Oliver Yes? Good.

He moves away.

And the old bike held out OK did she?

Becky Yes! She's brilliant.

Oliver Even up our horrible hill?

Becky She's amazing. I love her. Not sure about me though. My arse is killing me.

Oliver Not sure that's the bike.

Becky groans at his 'joke'.

That how you fuck your husband?

Becky No. I don't know. Probably not.

He sits. Lounges. Looks at her.

Oliver How do you feel? You feel OK?

Becky Well number one: I'm *starving*.

He laughs.

And also. I feel. Dunno. Like
    hugging a tree!

Oliver Really?

Becky Yeah. Ha. Like going into the woods naked! Or swimming in a river!

Oliver Wouldn't swim in the river round here.

Becky No?

Oliver Do you not remember when they found that hooker's body?

Becky No.

Oliver Yeah. Len whatsit found it one morning he was out fishing. Thought it was a mannequin. Got in. Touched it. Realised it was a body.

Becky That's horrible.

Oliver I know. Poor bastard. Had to have counselling.

Becky OK I won't swim in the river. But I might run in the woods naked.

Oliver Oh no. They found one in the woods too.

Becky Oh my God. Did they?

Oliver No.

She grimaces at him.

Sorry. I'm interrupting your enjoyable monologue about how fucking me has made you want to get back to nature. Carry on.

Becky Not nature exactly. Just yeah. I don't know. I just feel like myself again.

Oliver Are you not yourself then? With him?

Becky I am. I'm just
     I don't know. I'm one version of myself. And sometimes
     you know when you've been with someone a long time it's like
        it's hard to express sometimes
        other versions or
        I don't know.

Oliver I know what you mean.

Becky Yeah?

Oliver I look at my wife sometimes and I think yeah. You know. She's a good-looking woman. I've done OK. And then other times I think fucking hell. She's such a dog. Hasn't she let herself go? You know?

Becky Oh.

Oliver Imagine her as an old biddy with her face all

He pulls an 'old lady' face.

Becky But you love her though.

Oliver Course.

Becky That's good.

Oliver So you enjoyed yourself?

Becky Yeah.

Oliver Come here.

She goes to him.

Sit here.

She sits on him.

Not what you'd expect from a teacher is it?

He pulls her hair.

Becky Isn't it? Why?

Oliver Wouldn't expect a teacher to be such a dirty
little
bitch.

She giggles.

And you are definitely on the pill?

Becky I definitely won't get pregnant.

Oliver You really into all that stuff you were saying?

Becky Course.

Oliver Because
I mean if we keep it quiet
there's really no reason why we can't carry on till Alice
gets back. Act out a few of your more adventurous
fantasies.

Becky Really?

Oliver Just saying. I'm game. If you are. Though I do
have to preface it by saying I sort of promised Alice never
again so we'd have to be really careful.

Becky Oh.

Oliver She's a bit
  you know. Not unstable that's too strong a word but
  for all our sakes she can't find out. Sensitive. You know.

Becky I should probably go.

  She gets up.

Where are my knickers?

  Starts looking round the room.

Oliver Did I say something wrong?

Becky No! Not at all I just
  I told John I was out for a ride. I don't want him to
  worry.

Oliver You didn't lie then?

Becky I'm sorry?

Oliver It was a joke.

Becky No it's just he's paranoid.

Oliver In what way?

Becky Just

Oliver In a come round and kill me with an axe kind of
  way?

Becky In an over-protective way. Did you see where I put
  my knickers?

Oliver No.

Becky Do you do this all the time?

  Beat.

Oliver Does it matter?

Becky No. It's just
  it sounded like you did. I'm interested.

Oliver A few times. Not for ages. When I said never again
  I did mean it, I just
  you're a sexy girl.

Becky Yeah?

Oliver Yes.

Becky That's good. Where the fuck are my

  She finds them.

(aha!) No. I'm just asking because I don't want it to get messy. You know?

Oliver Oi.

Becky I have to be really careful.

  She is putting her knickers on.

Oliver Because you're a teacher?

Becky Because
  yes. And because of my husband.

Oliver I told you. I don't like mess. Leave your knickers off.

Becky You did say that. No. I'm going.

Oliver Come back tomorrow.

Becky Really?

Oliver Can you?

Becky Maybe.

Oliver Playing hard to get now?

He grabs her, her knickers are only half on. She keeps trying to pull them up.

Stop being all coy. Weren't all coy when you were begging me to come in your mouth were you?

Becky No.

Oliver I said stop it!

She stops. Stands there with her pants round her ankles.

Weren't all coy with my cock in your arse?

Becky No.

Oliver So what? Changed your mind?

Becky No!

Oliver This what you like?

Becky Yeah.

Oliver Give me those.

Becky What?

Oliver Give me your knickers.

Becky No. They're not clean.

Oliver I know.

Becky I can't ride a bike with no knickers.

Oliver Give them!

Becky Seriously Oliver, I'm not playing. I need them. And what if John sees?

She pulls her pants up.

Oliver Fair enough.

He pats her. She gets ready to leave.

It was lovely to see you. A nice surprise when you called.

78

Becky Yeah. Thanks for
you know.

   Beat.

Oliver See you tomorrow?

Becky I need to see how I feel. OK?

Oliver Sure. No pressure.

Becky No, it's nice. It's just. I don't know. When I see
John I –

Oliver Sure.

   Beat.

Just remember. It's good yeah? A bit of mystery.

THREE

Bakery Cottage. Morning.
   *John is sitting at the kitchen table assembling a baby's
mobile. Becky looks nice. She's getting ready to go out.*

John I've done it!

Becky What's that?

John The mobile your mother sent. Looks good. I can
get on with the painting now. Do you think the yellow or
the green? I think yellow. Green's a bit
isn't it. What do you think?

   She comes down the stairs.

Becky Are you talking about the nursery?

John I'm thinking yellow.

Becky If you want. I don't mind.

John Nice, no? And look!

He pulls a string on the mobile. It rotates, playing a little baby tune.

Becky It's lovely.

John Hang it in the window it'll catch the light. Make a rainbow.

Becky Why don't you take a break? Get out in the sun for a bit.

John Are you off?

Becky You've hardly been out the house all week. Yes.

John Well, we want it finished don't we? We're running out of time. Wait a second.

Becky I need to go.

John Two seconds. Come on. You haven't even looked at this! Look!

She stops. Turns. Looks at the mobile. Properly. He watches her. She smiles.

Becky It's beautiful.

John Your hair looks different.

She touches her hair. It is not different.

Becky No. I don't think so.

She laughs.

John I need to ask you something.

Becky What?

John I'm worried about something. You seem loads happier.

She laughs.

80

No that's good! I don't – just let me finish. And this past week
    things have been so much better between us. Haven't they?

Becky Yes?

John So I don't want to rock the boat. It's just

Becky What?

John The bike.

Becky What about it?

John It's good. I'm not saying it's not. It's just
    every day?

Becky I don't go every day.

John Nearly every day you do yes you do. And you go for hours. And you get home knackered. And I'm just
    I don't want to upset you because I'm really glad you're happy it's just I'm scared you might be overdoing it.

Becky John

John There was a thing on the telly yesterday about this woman
    she was pregnant
    and she fell off her bike
    and her baby died.

Becky What?

John It was on the telly.

Becky No it wasn't. What are you talking about?

John I don't remember. It was about all the bad things that can happen to women.

Becky I said I'd meet Jenny. Just
    try and get out the house for a bit.

On an impulse, she walks over to him. She kisses him on the head. Turns away.

I love you.

John I know.

Becky Now go on. Get some air. Go for a walk or something!

She is leaving.

John Don't go fast! Don't pedal hard!

But she is gone. He puffs in frustration. Runs to the door.

Don't go downhill!

He comes back in. He goes to the pipe. Checks it. Listens. There is no sound. He is confused.

FOUR

Hunter's Barn. Late afternoon. Birdsong.
Becky is dressed as a naughty teen. Knee-high socks. Short skirt. Perhaps a lollipop. Oliver is in his tracksuit trousers, smoking a spliff.

Oliver Does it hurt?

Becky Oh. My. God. Giving birth is going to be a piece of piss compared to that! I mean
    I just mean
    fuck me. When they rip the thing off it's like you can't even describe it.

Oliver Isn't he going to notice?

Becky I'll say it's for the summer. Because of the heatwave.

82

Oliver Everything's because of the heatwave. We can't help ourselves!

He waves his arms around.
  They laugh.

Want some?

He holds out the spliff. She thinks about it.

Becky Better not.

Oliver Good girl. Seriously though. Be careful.

Becky What do you mean?

Oliver Bikini line. Outfits. What's he going to say about all those marks? Won't he notice?

Becky No. He just thinks of me as a machine to make babies. An oven. You're a tool and I'm an oven.

Oliver He must be fucking insane. Look at you.

Becky When he does think about sex he just sticks a porn on. Honestly. He won't notice.

Oliver Why bother with porn when you've got the real thing right in front of you?

Becky Thanks.

Oliver Looks good though. Your pussy. Can't say it doesn't. Specially in the pictures.

Becky Did you like them?

Oliver What do you think?

Becky Don't show them to anyone!

Oliver Shit. Why didn't you say?

Becky What?

Oliver I forwarded them to Alice. She wanted to know what I've been up to.

Becky Ha ha. Don't! You scared me. John picked up my phone this morning when you texted? I thought I was going to have a heart attack.

Oliver Put me in as someone else.

Becky What do you mean?

Oliver In your phone. Save me as
Susie or whatever.

Becky It was a picture of your cock.

Oliver What did he look at it?

Becky No! I took it off him before he got chance.

Oliver But this is what I'm saying. You've got to be careful! Don't make him suspicious!

Becky Are you feeling guilty?

Oliver No. Are you?

Becky No. I mean
yes I feel guilty but I kind of feel guilty about everything anyway so

Oliver Do you?

Becky I haven't done my marking I haven't planned a lesson I haven't been to yoga I don't read enough I don't iron I'm ugly I'm fat I'm useless you know? Really it's just
one more thing to add to the list.

Oliver Tough gig. Being you.

Becky What about when she calls? You don't feel bad?

He thinks about this.

Oliver Yeah. But then I think
    what she doesn't know . . .
    and at the end of the day, we met. There was a
connection. Sure we could have ignored it. But then what?
What would be different?
    Nothing. We just
    wouldn't have done this.

Becky I guess.

Oliver So long as *we* both understand exactly what we're
doing
    and no one finds out
    what's the problem?

Becky There's this theory you know? That when people
have affairs
    they always want to get caught. Deep down. That's
what they want.

Oliver But this isn't an affair is it? We're just fucking.

    Becky nods.

I won't leave her.

Becky What?

Oliver Just so you know. I mean. I won't leave Alice.

Becky What made you say that?

Oliver Should say it, that's all.

Becky I don't want you to leave her.

Oliver That's good.

Becky Jesus.

Oliver Don't be like that.

Becky Like what?

Oliver I'm being up front with you. Don't / get all shirty.

Becky I'm just saying you don't (I'm not) you don't need to. I know!

Oliver OK, good.

Becky I hate this whole thing like
   women can't have sex without getting 'emotionally involved'. It's bullshit. I've had sex with loads of men and not given a shit afterwards.

Oliver Nice.

Becky No I just mean it's such a delusion. 'Oh you're so good Oliver I just can't help falling in love with you.'

Oliver I am good though.

Becky Fuck off.

Oliver Aren't I?

Becky Give me some of that.

   He hands her the spliff. She takes a big drag.

You think I'm this
   respectable
   married
   teacher person.

Oliver I really don't think you're that.

Becky Don't you?

   *He looks at her. Dressed as a teenager. Smoking a spliff.
   She giggles.*

What are we going to do next?

Oliver Thought we already said. Friday night.

Becky I know I mean after that.

86

Oliver After that we haven't got much time.

Becky I don't go back till September.

Oliver Alice is back next week.

Becky Oh. Well maybe that's good. John needs more help around the house. I've been neglecting him a bit so

Oliver Sure we can fit a little something in though can't we? What do you want to do?

Becky What about
with another girl?

Oliver Yeah?

Becky That's your top fantasy. Right?

Oliver Yeah.

Becky I like being your fantasy.

Oliver Ha.

Becky Could we do that?

Oliver Could do. If you know someone.

Becky I don't know someone. I thought we could
you know. Call somewhere. A website or something.

Oliver You gonna cough up?

Becky How much would it be?

Oliver Dunno.

Becky I could find out.

Oliver I might
know someone. Actually.

Becky Really?

Oliver You gonna get jealous?

Becky No!

Oliver Cos if you can't handle it we shouldn't do it.

Becky I can handle it. Why do you think I can't handle it? I can handle anything.

Oliver OK. Well. In that case yeah. I might know someone.

Becky Who is it?

Oliver Want me to set it up?

Becky So long as it's safe.

Oliver You might have to lend me fifty quid. I've uh lost my bank card. Gonna take a couple of weeks to get a new one.

Becky That's no problem. Set it up. When for?

Oliver You worry about Friday. Leave this one to me.

Becky OK. Cool.

Oliver Now sit on the chair. I want to fuck you again before you go.

Becky What time is it? I told John I was meeting Jenny.

Oliver We've got time.

Becky Tell me the time.

Oliver I'm not asking. Sit down.

Becky Or what?

Oliver Or else.

Becky Yeah?

She doesn't sit down.

Oliver Do as you're told. Sit down. Sit down!

She smiles at him.

SIT DOWN!

She sits down.

I'm practising for our next instalment. Open your legs.

Becky The only thing is

He grabs her face.

Oliver Open your legs bitch or I'll cut your throat!

Becky Hang on I'm just saying
about Friday
    I might have to bring John. To the thing. People have
been going on about it in the village apparently. He doesn't
want to miss out.

Oliver Yeah? Cool. Bring him.

Becky Really?

Oliver Bring him. Yes. We need the audience.

FIVE

Bakery Cottage. Night time.
    John is in bed reading Breastfeeding: The Essential
Guide. *He is talking to Becky, who is in the bathroom.*

John It was convincing but he made a bit of a meal of it.
All that moaning. Thought he'd really been stabbed for a
minute. Lying there writhing about I thought
    if he had been stabbed
    at what point would we realise? You know? Didn't
that happen once? Some comedian. Dropped dead and
everyone thought it was fake. I thought he was good
though. Your mate. Other than that I thought he was
pretty good. That car he drives is worth a fortune.

89

Beat.

Why are we still waiting for the plumber? I should have just done it myself.

Becky comes out. In her new nightie.

Becky We're waiting for the part. What time is it?

John I know we're waiting for the part. I'm saying why is it taking so long?

Becky They haven't made the noise for ages.

John They haven't made the noise. Doesn't mean it's fixed. If something makes a noise
 then stops making a noise
 that's when you should be really worried.

Becky I'm just going to do the kitchen.

John Leave it. I'll do it tomorrow.

Becky I want to wake up with it nice.

John I'll get up before you.

Becky No you won't and anyway I don't mind. I need something to do. You get in bed.

John Are you OK?

Becky Why wouldn't I be?

John You didn't enjoy it? This evening?

Becky It was fine. I just I wanted to get back.

John Lift up your thing. Let me look at Babooney.

Becky No!

John Look at your boobies. They're massive!

Becky Leave me alone.

John You can't keep hiding it you know. Once you start showing properly people are going to start coming up to you in the street. Trying to touch your belly.

Becky They fucking better not. I'll chop their hands off. Strangers touching me.

John It's nice isn't it?

Becky He was flirting with me. Didn't you notice?

John Who was?

Becky The bike man. Oliver. He followed us round the whole night. Put his hand on my arm about four times.

John I didn't notice.

Becky You don't notice anything. He could probably have groped my arse right in front of you, you wouldn't have done anything.

John Is that why you dragged us away?

Becky No, I dragged us away because I didn't want you to start talking to him about the state of my hormones. OK? Not everyone needs to know.

John Why not?

Becky Because it's none of his business!

John I didn't tell him!

Becky You were going to.

John How do you know he doesn't know? People know.

Becky People
don't really talk to him do they?

John I thought he was quite funny.

She stares at him.

What?

Becky So what you're mates with him now? After what I just said?

John What, that people don't like him?

Becky That he was flirting with me!

John I don't think he was.

Becky You think I'm making it up?

John No.

Becky So what if you'd seen?

John Well I would have said something. Obviously.

Becky Like what?

John I don't know. Probably just
    I mean it would depend.

Becky On what?

John On if it was making you uncomfortable. I mean if it was making you uncomfortable I don't know why you didn't say something yourself.

Becky Because I don't know. He's got a reputation hasn't he?

John Has he?

Becky As not very nice.

John Oh well in that case I probably wouldn't say anything. Just let him grope you!

He laughs.

I'm kidding! Come on love. I'm sorry if you felt weird. I just

92

honestly I thought he was a nice guy. If I got it wrong then

    cool. Next time we'll just avoid him. It's not like it's going to affect us in the village not being friends with him. Like you say, no one likes him anyway.

Becky Avoid him?

John Why not?
    What?
    What do you want me to say?

Becky What if I flirted back?

John Um. Well. Did you?

Becky No. I'm just saying what if I did?

John Well. You can flirt if you want. I trust you. Why would I care?

Becky Because maybe I want you to care.

John I don't mean I don't care! Course I care. Look at me!

Becky What?

John Care is all I ever do.

Becky stands for a moment, staring into space.

Becky?
    What going on in your head?
    Talk to me.

    Beat.

Baby?

Becky Why?

John Because
    I want to help.

Becky You can't help me.

John Where are you going?

Becky I'm going to sort the kitchen.

John OK. Well
go easy.

She heads down the stairs.

Love you!

Downstairs, she puts on an apron. Fluffs her hair.
Thinks of something, turns on the stereo. Radio Four
comes on, a low murmur. John picks up his book.
Yawns. She gets going on the kitchen.

Becky Shall I bring you a drink up?

John Yes please. Can I have a hot chocolate please?

Becky Be about ten minutes is that OK?

John Thank you sweetheart. You're an angel!

The door opens, a man in a balaclava enters. He is
holding a large knife. Becky jumps. Gasps. He puts a
finger to his lips. She nods. She will be quiet.
   He indicates she should move to the table. She does.
   He moves behind her. Roughly, he pushes up her
nightie, undoes his trousers. He puts the knife on the
table and grabs her face, covering her mouth. He
starts to have sex with her.
   As Becky and the intruder have sex, the gentle
strains of 'Sailing By', the tune for the Shipping
Forecast, waft from the stereo.
   Upstairs, John yawns. He is nearly falling asleep.
   Suddenly, Becky accidentally cries out. John wakes.

Did you say something, my love?

She grapples with the man, there is a struggle, she
manages to get her mouth free.

Becky No I just said
   did you say hot
   chocolate or Horlicks?

John Hot chocolate please. You OK down there?

Becky Yeah won't be long!

John Love you!

She turns back to the man. She nods.
   They carry on.
   The pipes groan and seem to shudder.

SIX

Hunter's Barn. Evening. Crickets chirp.
   Oliver reclines, drinking a glass of wine. Fanning
himself. Becky paces up and down.

Oliver You're making me hot. Sit down. Fuck's sake.

Becky Do you think she enjoyed it?

Oliver Did you enjoy it?

Becky I think she did. It's just weird because you can't
tell.

Oliver I could tell.

Becky How?

Oliver She made enough noise about it.

Becky She didn't really smile though. Did she?

Oliver She's Polish.

Becky Yeah but I mean. With a man. If a man doesn't
want to
   he just
   can't. Can he? Whereas with a girl –

Oliver People don't do things if they don't want to.

Becky Don't they?

Oliver What are you worried about? She got paid well enough. You know any teachers get fifty quid for an hour's work?

Becky No.

Oliver Fuck sight better than being an au pair. Wish I could have sex for my job. Sell my body. Bet I'd get shit loads.

Becky How did you know she'd be up for it?

Oliver I know she needs the money. And look at her.

   Becky laughs.

She's filth.

Becky I didn't expect her to be so soft. Am I that soft? She was so soft. I kept wanting to ask how old she was but I thought it was rude.

Oliver Twenty-four.

Becky Is she? She looks younger.

Oliver That's what she told me.

Becky That's OK then. Twenty-four's OK, isn't it? I mean do you think she knows
   I don't know

Oliver She knows.

Becky What?

Oliver What she's doing.

Becky There's nothing wrong with it is there? It's good to do these things isn't it? Have you know. Experiences. I think life is all about experiences. Don't you? I do!

Oliver Thought you said you could handle it.

Becky I am handling it!

Oliver Can you sit down please?

Becky I love being your fantasy. It's never been like this before. For me. You know? Ever. Has it for you?

Oliver I've enjoyed myself. Yeah. It's been fun.

Becky looks at him.

What?

Becky Why did you say it like that? 'It's been fun.'

Oliver Well Alice is back in a couple of days. So

Becky Is she?

Oliver You know that.

Becky Do I?

Oliver And you don't need to look all tragic. I'm not dying. We can always pick it up again next time she goes away.

Becky When will that be?

Oliver Dunno. October maybe?

Becky Too late. October's too late.

Oliver For what?

Becky For me.

Oliver Calm down.

Becky I forgot. I forgot she was coming back. It's like it just

She waves her arms.

out of my mind.

Oliver OK stop now. Stop it! Remember what we said? You've been good all summer. Don't piss me off right at the last minute being silly.

Becky Won't you miss me?

Oliver I'll miss fucking you.

He laughs.

OK. Sorry. I'll probably miss you a bit. But I'll survive.

Becky All I mean is, do you do this with your wife? All this? Do you do this with your wife?

Oliver Course not.

Becky So yes see this is what I'm saying it's like this whole
    part of you gets squashed or
    hidden or
    'not allowed'. Don't you think? What if we could have both?

Oliver I don't want this with my wife.

Beat.

Becky What?

Oliver She's my wife.

Beat.
    Becky shakes her head.

Becky Don't call me up in three months' time saying you made a mistake.

Oliver I won't.

Becky It has to be now.

Oliver 'It's now or never.'

Becky Yes!

Oliver What happened to 'I don't get involved after sex?' Eh?

Becky Who said that? / I didn't say that.

Oliver You did.

Becky No I didn't.

Oliver Word for word . 'No, Oliver, you just think that cos you've got such a big ego.'

Becky I didn't mean it like that.

Oliver It's what you said.

Becky You said we were just fucking! What did you want me to say?

Oliver Nothing. The less you say the better. I don't know why we're even having this conversation.

Becky Because I need to tell you something.

Oliver Tell you what, I'll lend you my phone. You can call someone who gives a shit.

He laughs.

OK that was an old one.

Becky It's just
I just

She tries to say something. But he is losing his patience.

Oliver Fuck's sake Becky. Spit it out. What?

Beat.

Becky I need to see you before she gets back. Don't
just
one more time. Please?

Oliver I'm too old for this.

Becky OK. OK. In that case
Let me send you something.

Oliver Whatever.

Becky Can I still send you something?

Oliver Do what you want. OK?

Becky And if you change your mind

Oliver I won't.

Becky But if you change your mind
just
give me a call.

The sound of wind.

SEVEN

Bakery Cottage. Afternoon. Wind gusts against the windows.
Becky is sitting at the kitchen table, playing with her phone. There is a toolbox on the kitchen floor, near a section of pipe. A shiny new pipe has been fitted, and the old pipe lies nearby.
From the phone, the sound of people having sex.

Becky What are you doing in there? For God's sake.

The door opens to the upstairs bathroom.
Mike emerges. He is in his briefs.

Mike Did you say something?

Becky Doesn't matter.

Mike I wasn't going to flush in case you need to go before we turn the water on. But then I thought
well I put the thingy in there so I thought

Becky What are you talking about?

Mike The condom.

Becky Oh.

Mike Hear that wind? Heat's gonna break, don't you think?

He is heading downstairs.

Can't keep on like this. Oh. Great. You worked it out then?

She ignores him.

What's it look like?

Becky It's a good camera.

Mike I'm a good cameraman.

He tries to kiss her. She pulls away.

Becky Don't.

Mike That your thing is it? Watching it after?

Becky Maybe.

Mike Never tried it like that.

Becky Oh well.

Mike New thing for me that.

Becky You should get dressed.

Mike What are you doing?

Becky Nothing.

Mike Looked like you were sending it.

Becky No just
yes. To myself.

Mike With a video?

Becky Yes.

Mike Clever.

Becky I'm worried about the time. Can you please get dressed?

Mike Sorry. Course. / Sorry.

Becky Sorry
  I just

Mike No you're OK. I should get dressed. You know what? These
  are my lucky pants. Can you believe that? I don't usually wear them on a Friday but I couldn't find the Friday pair this morning so I had to use the Saturday pair. And the pair I would've put on – well! If I'd've been wearing those I think I'd've turned you down, love. Not that I'd've wanted to. Not dirty! I don't mean dirty. Just, full of holes. Couldn't've let you see me in those. Dear oh dear. I said to myself not that long ago it was I said, 'Mike? It's just as well you're on your own mate cos if anyone saw the state of your underwear they'd run a mile off.' Only
  now I'm telling you which I don't know why I'm doing so

Becky I'm sure it's fine.

Mike Don't want you thinking I've let myself go.

Becky I mean
  it doesn't really matter what I think does it?

Mike Does to me.

Becky It doesn't. OK? It doesn't matter to me so it shouldn't matter to you.

Mike Well that's very kind of you love, but I want to look nice for you.

Becky I'm married. Right? I'm going to have a baby.

Mike Right you are.

Becky I'm sorry.

Mike No no. My mistake.

Becky It's OK.

Mike My apologies.

Becky No need.

Mike Put my things on.

Becky Thanks.

Mike (*as he dresses*) Did I tighten the new bit of pipe?

Becky I don't know.

Mike You caught me off guard. Halfway through. Remind me to check before I go.

Becky OK.

   Silence till he finishes dressing. When he is dressed:

John's hung this mobile in the spare room. Clowns and little animals. I just keep thinking
   what if I can't look after it?

   Beat.

I'm sorry about your wife.

   Beat.

I want you to go now.

   Mike looks at her.

Mike Could we

Becky Just make an invoice. I'll get John to pay.

Mike OK.

Becky If you tell John he'll kill me. You've seen the marks.

Mike I won't.

Becky You promise?

Mike I promise.

Becky Thank you.

Mike You sure you're OK?

Becky I don't know.

Mike Shouldn't let him do that. You know? It's not right.

Becky It's my choice. Oh!

She holds her stomach.

Mike Is it the baby?

Becky I thought

Suddenly Jenny springs in through the back door, as if carried on a gust of wind. She is holding aloft a baby bouncer with an air of triumph.

Jenny Hello there? Blimey O'Reilly! It's windy out there! Hello darling. Oh hello Mike!

Beat.

Becky Hi!

Jenny How are we all?

Mike Morning Mrs Leger.

Jenny God it had my skirt up over my head about five times on the way over. Poor Len Gogherty got a right eyeful. Sorry Mike. Too much information. Are you OK darling? You look dreadful.

Becky I'm fine. Are you OK?

Mike She's not feeling well.

Jenny What is it? Are you bleeding?

Becky No. No, I'm fine I'm just
   morning sickness.

Jenny Are you sure? There's no blood. Do you want to go and check?

Becky Not really. Are you
   did you just come from outside?

Jenny What do you mean? Course I did.

Becky I don't know.

Jenny I think you should go and check your knickers darling you look very pale.

Becky I don't want to check my knickers.

Jenny Run and check. I'll / look after Mike.

Becky I don't want to check.

Jenny Sometimes you can't feel it.

Becky OK I'll check.

Becky puts her hands between her legs and checks for blood.

Jenny Oh!

Becky brings her hand out. Shows Jenny.

Becky OK? It's fine.

Jenny Glass of water!

Mike Oh / there's

Becky I don't want a glass of water.

   Jenny tries the tap.

Mike Water's off. Sorry. I'll do it on my way.

Jenny If you could Mike I think Becky needs a glass of
water.

Mike Right you are. Well.
   How's your boiler?

Jenny It's wonderful thank you Mike. Not that we need
it in this weather eh?

Mike On it's way out I reckon. Can't keep on how we
have been.

Jenny Absolutely. I mean. Gusty.

Mike Right then.

Becky Are you off?

Mike I'm off. I'll er
   see you soon?

Becky Call John about the money.

Mike Will do.

   Mike stands for a moment.

Jenny You OK Mike?

Mike I just wanted to say
   thank you for letting me mend your pipes. I had a
really good time.

Becky OK.

Mike See you.

He leaves. As he opens the door, the wind blows back through. Jenny holds on to her hair.
  When he is gone, Jenny laughs.

Jenny What the hell? Are you OK? What's going on?

Becky Nothing.

  The pipes start to groan.

Jenny I don't believe you. What are you doing just sitting at the table with
  him and not feeling well you should've called me!

  Suddenly the sink tap shoots water.

Sorry. I must have
  here

  Jenny turns the tap down. Fills a glass of water.

Here you go.

  Becky takes a sharp breath.
    Jenny sits.

You seem
  not OK.

Becky I'm just

Jenny Is it something I said?

Becky What? No.

Jenny Have I done something?

Becky No. Course not. I just

Jenny Where's John?

Becky At a fatherhood workshop.

Jenny Is everything OK?

Becky Did you see something?

Jenny When?

Becky Doesn't matter.

Jenny Did he
did Mike
what did he do?

Becky Nothing.

Jenny What did he do?

Becky Nothing! I promise.

Jenny If he did / something –

Becky Jenny. Listen to me. It was nothing. I'm OK.
I promise. I just feel a bit sick.

Jenny If you're sure.

Becky I'm sure.

Jenny I brought you the bouncer!

Becky Thanks.

Jenny Having a break. From the chaos.

Jenny drinks the water.

Sorry.

Becky It's fine.

Jenny I think I need

Beat.

Becky What?

Jenny I can't remember.

Jenny puts her face in her hands. Peers up at Becky.

I thought
if you wanted. You could come over? Let me return
the favour. Dinner. I can shove the kids in bed. Dose them
up with a bit of Calpol?

Becky Where's Jules?

Jenny laughs.

Jenny Where's Jules? Where's Jules? It's like the chorus of my life! God knows. Tanzania? Afghanistan? Somewhere terrible. Somewhere he can do some good. Somewhere people are worthy of him. And where isn't Jules? Where is Jules *never*? Here. At home. With us. And you know why? Because no one thinks that's anything special do they? Me. Sitting at home. Going crazy. Being told I'm an idiot by a *five-year-old boy*. I've got a PhD in Theoretical Astrophysics but oh no! I'm just stupid old Mummy!

Becky Um. Where are the boys?

Jenny I've locked them in a cupboard. With gags on. HA! Not really. They're in front of the telly watching *Countdown*. Sebastian just got an eight-letter word. It made me want to kill myself. Will you come over? Please? I haven't seen you for weeks. Where have you been?

Becky I just
I don't know. I don't feel very well.

Jenny Please Becky? I think I might do something bad.

Becky Like what?

Jenny Like call Monika. Ask her to come back.

Becky Don't do that! Just. Call your mum. Call – Juliet or someone. I'll come and see you tomorrow. I promise. I just can't now.

Jenny Please?

Becky I can't.

Jenny Why not?

Becky I need a shower.

Jenny Have one at mine.

Becky I just
want to be on my own for a bit.

Jenny Oh.

Becky I'm sorry.

Jenny It doesn't matter.

Becky Jenny

Jenny Honestly. Sorry to be a pain.

Becky You're not.

Jenny I am. I nag and I fuss and I'm stupid. That's what you think. It's what they all think. And you're right. It must be true!

She goes to the door. Opens it. The wind blows through.

It must be true if you all think it!

Becky Jenny –

Jenny closes the door.
The pipes groan and shudder.
Becky opens the door. Grit blows in her eyes.

Shit. Ow.

She presses her hands to her eyes.

Jenny!

She gives up. Goes back to the table. Drinks some of the water. Blinks till she can see.
Grabs her phone off the side. As she talks, she makes herself ready to leave.

Hi. It's me. Did you get it? I feel weird. Are you home? I need to talk to you. It's important. I'm sorry. I know we said we wouldn't do this it's just

I can't
I feel
I just
need to see you. I'll explain when I get there.

She looks around. And leaves the house.
   The sun goes behind a cloud. The room darkens.
Suddenly, the new part of the pipe, untightened, pops
free.
   A gush of gloopy, thick, dirty water shoots out of
the pipe and over the floor.

EIGHT

Hunter's Barn. Late afternoon. Heavy, yellow light. Wind
gusts.
   Becky, still in her nightie. Sweating. Alice, smart
casual, is beaming.

Alice Sorry about the mess. I'm still on New York time.
Haven't quite got my head around sorting the house.

Becky No not at all. I'm sorry to just – turn up like this.

Alice Do you know what it is yet?

Becky Oh. I mean. Not yet. We've got
   a scan. In a few weeks.

Alice Do you want to know? Or do you want a surprise?

Becky Don't know. I'm so sorry about this. I saw you
through the window I thought you were Oliver. I mean.
Not that it matters I just

Alice Do people treat you different?

Becky Sorry?

Alice I'm in this forum. Fertility. You know. Sit in
meetings on my BlackBerry secretly chatting with all

these women all over the country. One of them finally did it. Reckons people smile at her in the street for the first time in her life. Women especially. Do they smile at you?

Becky I haven't noticed. Maybe.

Alice You're sweating.

Becky The hill. The wind was against me.

Alice You shouldn't really, you know.

Becky It's fine. Exercise is good.

Alice Oliver didn't mention you were having a baby.

Becky Really?

Alice No.

Becky What did he say?

Alice Well apparently I didn't leave him enough pocket money so he sold you my bike. And then he had to fix it.

Becky He was great.

Alice And you came to see his Dick
  Turpin?

Becky Right.

Alice Funny what men omit. I've always thought that. My mother used to complain about my father she'd send him down the pub to find out all the gossip and he'd come back and say so-and-so's fucking so-and-so's husband but that was all he knew. Never got the details. So vague, see? Whereas my mother was one for details.

Somewhere outside, a low rumble of thunder.

I'm the same. I notice everything. Sounds like the weather's going to break at last.

Becky I just wanted a quick word about the handlebars.

Alice Of course. I'm so sorry. I'll get him for you. Oh. It's not his I suppose?

Becky What?

Alice Your child. It's not my husband's?

Becky No!

Alice I'm teasing.

Becky What?

   Alice laughs.

Alice Is it weird to see me in person?

Becky I'm sorry?

Alice You know. When you hear about someone or know they exist. Or you've seen them in a photo say. It's weird then
  to see them in person. To realise
  that's an actual human being. You know? Not just a a not just someone in a video.

Becky I haven't seen you in a video.

Alice No. Sorry. I'm not being clear. I was talking about that video of you.

  Beat.

I'll get Olly.

  Alice leaves.
    Becky stands. Unable to move. She shakes her head. She takes a sharp breath. She is finding it hard to breathe.
    The sound of feet thudding down stairs.
    She braces herself.
    Oliver enters. Quietly furious.

Oliver What did I tell you?

Becky I did call.

Oliver Did I call you back?

Becky I'm sorry. I didn't know what else to do.

Oliver We had a deal.

Becky I don't know where else to go.

Oliver Go home!

Becky I can't!

Oliver Go to your friend's.

Becky You're my friend. Please Oliver? Just
    Please? Can't you
    I'm not trying to make trouble I just
    after everything, I thought

Oliver Now you listen to me

   He grabs her by the arm.

we had some fun. And that's it. Right? I'm not saying
never again but this is not part of the deal. Now I'm
sorry. But you need to go. OK?

Becky The video.

Oliver What about it?

Becky You didn't – what did you do with it?

Oliver Nothing. What do you mean?

Becky I just I mean did you watch it?

Oliver Uh. Yes. Some of it. I got distracted. Alice called
me in for lunch.

Becky Did you like it?

Oliver To be honest Becky
    I didn't really think about it. OK?

Becky Oh.

Oliver Hey. You listen to me now. You wanted to do it. You did that for yourself. Don't even try and make me feel responsible.

Becky I thought it might change your mind.

Oliver Did you? That was a bit stupid wasn't it?

Becky I didn't like it.

Oliver No? Looked like you were enjoying yourself to me.

Becky Did it?

Oliver Weren't you?

Becky I can't
    I can't get rid of it.

Oliver Then you shouldn't have done it.

   The thunder again. A bit louder.

Becky We've got something.

Oliver I'm married.

Becky I love you.

Oliver Here we go.

Becky We've got a connection. You said it yourself!

Oliver It was just pretend.

Becky I don't believe you. This is real. I feel it. When I'm with you
    it's OK to be who I really am.

Oliver Sweetheart. Go home.

Becky Come away with me.

Oliver Go home Becky.

Becky Get away from all this. Leave it behind. Somewhere nice. Somewhere hot. Somewhere far away. There's no going back. I know. I know. But if you be with me. It makes it OK. I need you to make it OK. Please Oliver. / Please

Oliver Shut up / now please.

Becky please Oliver

He grabs her arm. She cries out.

careful be
    careful with me!

He lets go.

Oliver I said shut UP!

Becky Please

Oliver Now you listen to me you fucking moron. You get out of my house and don't come back and if you speak to me again or contact me again or make any attempt to tell my wife
    if you say a word
    to anyone. About any of this? I will show that video of you
    a school teacher
    fucking that poor old plumber
    to everyone in the village. OK? And you'll probably lose your husband. And you'll definitely lose your job. And if you stay in this village
    which I doubt you'd be able to do but if you do you'll spend your whole life being whispered about. And laughed at. And don't expect anyone to feel sorry for you. Because they won't. You know what they'll say?

They'll say silly fucking bitch. Stupid slag. She got what she deserved.

A crash of thunder. Rain pours.

NINE

Birdleigh Hill. Dusk.
  Becky rides her bike down the hill in the rain. Faster and faster. The wind is behind her. Lightning flares and thunder crashes.
  She lets go with one hand.
  She lets go with the other. The bicycle veers dangerously. Skids. She is going to fall.

TEN

Bakery Cottage. Night time. Heavy rain.
  Jenny is cleaning the floor.
  The pipe has dripped dry.
  Becky is in bed, wrapped in a blanket. Her face is grazed.
  John is downstairs talking to Jenny. He is making them all tea.

John Just waltzes out the house and leaves it essentially like a death trap do you know what I mean? Be careful. It's hot.

Jenny Thanks, John.

John Of all the days. You know? I get that phone call. I have to go to the hospital. Pick up my wife. I'm already planning to go round and murder that bastard in Birdleigh who sold her the bike and we get home to this. And if Mike thinks I'm not going to tell people then he's wrong.

You know? Job like that you're made on your reputation. Jenny honestly, you don't have to do that.

Jenny I feel awful. It's my fault. I recommended him!

John You weren't to know.

Jenny It's done now, anyway.

John Thanks Jenny. Thanks for coming over. Thanks.

Jenny Don't be ridiculous. Times like this. You need your friends don't you?

John You appreciate the value of living in a community. It's true. A place where people look out for each other.

Jenny And besides. You know. It puts things in perspective doesn't it? I've been sitting round complaining about about about not having an au pair and you're here you could have lost your baby.

John When they were putting the jelly on. Waiting for the machine to pick it up. I was just standing there thinking you know
    just this whole
    you know
    of
    that. Because
    it's just because it's because it's
    my baby.

Jenny I know.

John I was so angry and then we heard its heart and

He nods firmly.

on the machine

He keeps nodding.

Jenny Did she seem
    I mean she must have been relieved?

John I wish I could have a baby. You know? I'd love to have it.

Jenny Course you would.

John I said that. I said Becky, I'd love to be the one who has to have it. But I can't.

Jenny John darling I've got my socks wet. Have you got a plastic bag I can take them home in?

John Sure. Somewhere. I mean I try not to use them but

He starts to look.

sometimes things are unfair. You know? We all have different gifts. We have to use them to the best of our ability. She does keep them here somewhere. You can't always just have things the way you want.

Jenny The main thing is we're all safe. We're all OK.

He opens the plastic-bag cupboard. Tesco bags pile out on his head.

John Aha! Oh!

Jenny Great!

John I don't believe this. What the fuck? Where the hell have all these come from?

Jenny Tesco?

John BECKY?

Jenny John – she's

John No I don't care. This is one step too far. This is the last bloody straw this is!

He heads up the stairs. Bags in hand.

Jenny John?! No!

John Becky?

Becky What?

John What the fuck is this?

Becky What?

John You been going to Tesco behind my back?

Becky No.

John I don't fucking believe you Becky. You know how much this means to me. What have you bought?

Becky I don't

John No come on.

Becky It was ages ago. / I haven't done it for ages.

John Oh really? Because this one's got a receipt in and and and look!
   Ha!

Becky John.

John Thursday. Is it? Friday. This Friday. Bread. Olive oil. Carrots. Broccoli. Chicken?

Becky Please

John Was it free range?

Becky I don't

John You've bought fucking shit chicken from the *supermarket*?

Becky I'm / sorry.

John Do you know what they do to that meat? Do you know how they treat it?

Becky I know.

John No. You don't. That's exactly the point. It could come from anywhere. Anywhere.

Becky I'm sorry.

John What else? Celery. Basmati rice. Condoms. Brie.

She freezes.
The tiniest of moments. Tiny. Almost not a moment.

Becky That was for . . . John –

John Did you eat it?

Becky What?

John The brie. Where is it?

Becky I don't know. In the cheese thing.

John Brie is a soft cheese!

Becky I had a craving!

John Why didn't you tell me?

Becky I don't know.

John You make a fool of me. You know that? I make this big thing in the village about how important it is to do all this stuff. You know? I can't help being someone who cares about the planet. I just do. I see someone with a plastic bag it tears me up inside. You know? People in this country are so lucky. Any time we want. We can have anything we want. It just seems like a small sacrifice to me to shop locally and use a Bag for Life. And when I'm saying this sort of thing to people I want them to respect me. I want them to listen and I think they do listen and I think they do respect me and the thing is
    if they then see *you*
     prancing round the village with a plastic bag from Tesco crammed full of battery-farmed eggs and awful cheapskate chicken

what are they going to think of me? Eh? What are they going to think?

Becky I'm sorry. I said I was sorry. I'm sorry. I won't do it again. I promise. I promise.

He sits on the edge of the bed. For a moment, they are both at a loss.

John Is there something going on?

Becky No.

John Because you seem
funny.

Becky No.

John You've seemed funny for a while. Actually. And I've been telling myself it's hormones but now I'm thinking maybe it's something else.

Pause.

And I just want you to know that you can tell me. You know? Whatever it is. I'm sure we can work it out.

Pause.

There's nothing so bad we can't get over. Is there?

Becky It isn't anything.

John Is it because of the bedroom thing?

Becky What?

John 'Sex'.

Becky No.

John I know it's upset you, me being
you know but I just wanted to say

Becky It's fine. I've changed my mind.

John Really?

Becky I've gone off it.

John Oh.

Becky I don't want to again. Not ever. It's disgusting.
It disgusts me. Uch!

> *Her body reacts to the thought of it.*

Disgusting! I don't want to think about it.

John Oh.

Becky So don't worry about it. I won't try and make you
do it again.

John No it's fine. I mean. It's probably
you know

Becky It's not hormones.

John OK.

Becky I mean it. I just want things back to how they
were before. Before
before before the holidays.

> *He laughs.*
> *He kisses her.*

John I'd better see if Jenny's OK.

Becky You're a good man.

John I do my best.

> *He sees the 'Wedding Crockery: Spare' box. The DVDs
> scattered around it. He has a thought. Starts to collect
> them into the box.*

Have a little tidy quickly.

Becky Yeah. Might close my eyes for a bit.

John Good idea.

He picks up the box. Stands.

I'll bring your tea up.

Becky What happened to my bike?

John Oh that. Stupid thing. We should have got you a
new one from town not some bloody
    second-hand
    shagged-out old trash.

Becky Where is she?

John *She*
    is out there in the dark
    rusting. *She*
    is lucky I didn't dump her in the river. *She*
    can fucking rot for all I care. And I hope that Birdleigh
idiot drives past and sees her all mangled and abandoned
on the side of the road. Fucking
    wanker. Sorry.

    Beat.

Sorry my love.

Becky You won't leave me will you? Whatever happens.
Please. Don't leave me.

John Shush now! Stop being silly. Lie down. I'll get your
tea. Do you want a biscuit?

Becky No thanks.

John Organic custard cream?

Becky I'm OK.

John Right you are. Gonna take these bitches downstairs.
Put them out of the way.

    He goes downstairs.

In the bed, Becky stays very very still. As though, if she moves, something will break.

Downstairs, Jenny is sitting at the table. John puts the box of DVDs back in the empty Tesco cupboard.

Jenny She OK?

John Yeah. She's great.

He closes the cupboard. He picks up a tea.

I feel like
    this is going to sound soppy but. Yeah. I feel like I've
got her back. Hopefully now we can get back to normal.

ELEVEN

13 Dog Lane. Night time. Rain.
    Alone, Mike watches the video of him fucking Becky.
    Mike wanks.

The End.